Consent Issues and Complications in Obstetrics and Gynaecology

Consent Issues and Complications in Obstetrics and Gynaecology

Authors

Prabha Sinha, FRCOG, MRCPI
Consultant in Obstetrics and Gynaecology,
Conquest Hospital, St Leonards-on-Sea,
East Sussex, UK

Mamta Mishra, MRCOG
Obstetrician and Gynaecologist

Published by:
Anshan Ltd
11a Little Mount Sion
Tunbridge Wells
Kent. TN1 1YS

Tel: +44 (0) 1892 557767
Fax: +44 (0) 1892 530358

e-mail: info@anshan.co.uk
website: www.anshan.co.uk
© 2012 Anshan Ltd

ISBN: 978 1 848290 46 4

The use of registered names, trademarks, etc, in this publication does not imply, even in the absence of a specific statement that such names are exempt from the relevant laws and regulations and therefore for general use.

While every effort has been made to ensure the accuracy of the information contained within this publication, the publisher can give no guarantee for information about drug dosage and application thereof contained in this book. In every individual case the respective user must check current indications and accuracy by consulting other pharmaceutical literature and following the guidelines laid down by the manufacturers of specific products and the relevant authorities in the country in which they are practicing.

British Library Cataloguing in Publication Data
A catalogue record for this book is available from the British Library.

Copy Editor: Catherine Lain
Cover Design: Emma Randall
Cover Image: Shutterstock
Typeset by: Emma Randall
Printed and bound by: Lavenham Press

Contents

Appendices

Preface

Increased litigation can be partly blamed on the changing healthcare system. Patients and society as a whole are strongly ambivalent about doctors. Some of the blame for the declining public esteem of physicians lies at the door of managed care. We may be viewed as invulnerable healers with 'godlike decision-making powers' or as quacks out to make a buck, or anywhere in between.

As we can see from the 1620 epigram by John Owen this ambivalence is not new:

> "God and the Doctor we alike adore
> But only when in danger, not before
> The danger is o'er, both are alike requited,
> God is forgotten, and the Doctor slighted."

Patients expect health professionals to be available whenever they need us. They like us to have plenty of time to listen to their concerns and always be in a good mood, no matter how exhausted we are. All of us are supposed to be infallible in diagnosis and treatment and to be paragons of virtuous behaviour in our communities. We may realise these expectations are unrealistic, but nonetheless they can cause considerable stress.

We are limited in what we can do about today's healthcare environment. But we can stand up against the winds of change by altering our outlooks, our lifestyles (by preventing stress and occupational hazards) and ourselves.

In addition to the pressure from society and patients, stress can be self-induced, stemming from the very qualities that make doctors good at their job. Doctors are empathic, which can lead to over involvement with patients. They are conscientious and tend to overwork themselves; our 'shadow' is self-doubt, accounting for the compulsion to read and attend courses and learn new technology.

Increasing litigation and growing government intrusion into the practice of our profession causes pressure and is demoralising to the healthcare professionals. In addition, escalating practice costs, the simultaneous and almost contradictory expectation that we stay up-to-date and always provide high-quality care, coupled with declining esteem in the eyes of the public, all cause a great deal of stress and uneasiness among doctors.

List of Figures/Tables

About the Authors

Prabha Sinha is a Consultant Obstetrician and Gynaecologist at the Conquest Hospital in St Leonards-on-Sea, East Sussex, UK. She is also Honorary Consultant in Fetal Medicine at Guy's and St. Thomas' Hospitals in London. She has Fellowship of the Royal College of Obstetricians and Gynaecologists (FRCOG) and Membership of the Royal College of Physicians of Ireland (MRCPI). She is involved with undergraduate students from Brighton and GKT Medical School, as well as postgraduate education and assessment. She is currently an examiner for the Membership of the Royal College of Obstetricians and Gynaecologists (MRCOG), as well as the GMC exam for overseas doctors. She has also been a teacher on MRCOG courses locally, nationally, at the RCOG and internationally.

She has published many articles in peer reviewed journals and made a huge number of presentations and lectures in various national and international conferences.

She has written EMQ books for MRCOG Parts 1 and 2, DRCOG and OSCE for Colposcopy.

This is her ninth authored book.

Matma Mishra is a member of the Royal College of Obstetricians and Gynaecologists (MRCOG) with ten years of experience in obstetrics and gynaecology. She has a great interest in teaching and training and participates in organizing and running MRCOG Part 1 and 2 courses twice a year in New Delhi.

Acknowledgements

I am very grateful to Diana Hamilton-Fairley for her initial construct of the book and advice on the layout and to Debbie Williams, Steve Vlismas, Namita Unni, Annette Schriener, Mr Argent and all those who provided me with practical advice and for reading through the manuscript.

I am very grateful to Jenny Turner and Margaret Ellis (Rosewell Library) for their help in initial proof-reading.

Introduction

In recent years a lot of emphasis has been placed on obtaining consent for surgical and medical procedures to avoid litigation and associated escalating cost. This has become an integral part of clinical risk management and clinical governance in the current NHS.

The NHS was established in 1948 to provide comprehensive free medical care to all. Over the years, especially in the last two decades, there has been a veritable mountain of complaints following trends in the USA.

Approximately 350 maternity claims are filed with the NHSA every year. Since 1995, 61% of these have related to claims arising out of birth. In 2007–2008 the total cost of Clinical Negligence Scheme for Trusts maternity claims was £163 million.[1]

The total cost to this country of all litigation is £10 billion a year or about 1% of GDP, and is increasing by 15% annually. Almost half of it is lawyer's fees and administrative costs.

The cost to the NHS is accelerating at a similar rate. The payouts, including both completed cases and continuing payments, was expected to pass £800 million in 2009 – a 60% rise on five years previously. When settlements relating to staff injuries are included, the total is even higher.[2] This situation puts extra pressure on the NHS. Therefore, it is even more important to save costs by minimising risks and negligence.

Problems relating to consent are the reason for a great proportion of medico-legal claims. Adequate, informed consent and better record keeping of all communications will avoid a lot of complaints and litigation.

This book is a new edition, which has been updated to reflect recent changes in consent issues. It is designed to help in obtaining consent for common procedures undertaken in obstetrics and gynaecology. It is intended not only for doctors but also for midwives, nursing staff, medical students and other health professionals. It is also for overseas doctors who are new and generally less familiar to the risk management, clinical governance and litigation system in the United Kingdom. They have to learn the practice of this country quickly and obtaining consent is a very important aspect to it. All in all, whatever the position, the health professional has to ensure that he or she is well versed in the art and science of obtaining informed consent and proper communication.

This book aims to help to understand the types of consent, how to obtain consent and its medico-legal implications when things go wrong. Medicine can never be free of mishaps. Sadly, the current medical culture is one where error is considered synonymous with incompetence or negligence. Most procedures carry recognised complications. Despite being carried out by the most skilful and experienced operator, it is very important to prime the patient (and/or the family) about the consequences that may occur as a result of a particular procedure. It is very important that the patient and her family are fully aware of possible complications. This not only prepares everyone in case something goes wrong, but also takes away the often repeated claim that 'I was not told about this or I would not have had this operation'.

A very important aspect of the consent process is for the practitioner to know thoroughly the procedure or investigation, especially the details and complications. Most of the litigation involved is due to either dissatisfaction with the results, or complications that ensue following operations. It is consequently very important that we know about the process before we meet the patient. This book attempts to serve as a ready guide for a practitioner.

Consent Issues and Complications in Obstetrics and Gynaecology is not a substitute for a clinical textbook but instead provides an invaluable on-the-spot reference for various operations and their complications, ways and means of minimising risk, and dealing with difficult situations. So, the complications especially are covered in great detail.

References

1. *Written Evidence from Sands (CAL 38)*
   http://webcache.googleusercontent.com/search?q=cache:D8s_sjr
   atlkJ:www.publications.parliament.uk/pa/cm201012/cmselect/cmh
   ealth/786/786we26.htm+obstetric+and+gynaecology+litigation+cl
   aim+in+UK&cd=15&hl=en&ct=clnk&gl=uk&source=www.google.c
   o.uk (accessed 16/9/11). December 2010.
2. Lister S. Lawyers growing rich on NHS negligence. *The Times.*
   December 18, 2009.

CHAPTER 1: THE BURDEN AND LITIGATION OF OBSTETRICS AND GYNAECOLOGY

Obstetric negligence is one of the major causes of clinical negligence litigation. Errors and misdiagnosis in obstetric care can result in catastrophic outcomes, with injuries being sustained by both the mother, the baby and even causing death to either or both the mother and baby. Nearly 77% of obstetricians and gynaecologists have been sued at least once, and 50% more than three times.[1]

Obstetric negligence cases are extremely complex in terms of both the legal complications and the stressful situation. Such cases are emotional and very painful experiences for all those healthcare professionals involved.

Some injuries are unavoidable and a number of them are caused by so-called negligence. Important birth injuries include:
- Cerebral Palsy
- Erb's Palsy (brachial plexus injury/shoulder dystocia)
- injuries to the mother (perineal trauma)
- brain injuries
- fractured/broken bones.

The main cause of obstetric injuries is frequently found to be the mismanagement of the pregnancy and/or the labour. Therefore, it is critical for midwives, obstetricians and other clinicians to identify obstetric abnormalities at an early stage and respond to them within an appropriate period to minimise the risk of obstetric negligence claims.
The speciality of obstetrics and gynaecology is sued more frequently than any other after general surgery (Figure 1).

However, money claimed by obstetrics and gynaecology supersedes that of any other speciality (Figure 2).

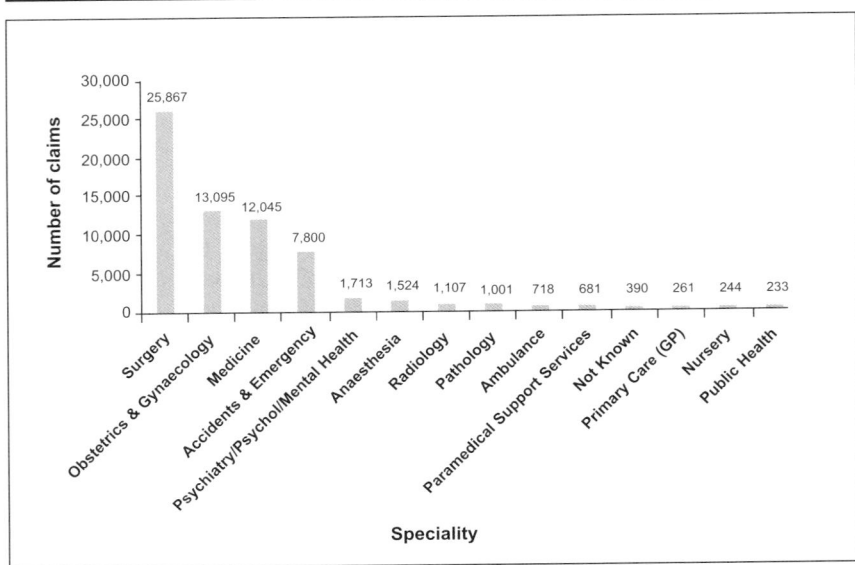

Figure 1: Total number of reported CNST claims by specialty as at 31/03/11 (© NHSLA)[2]

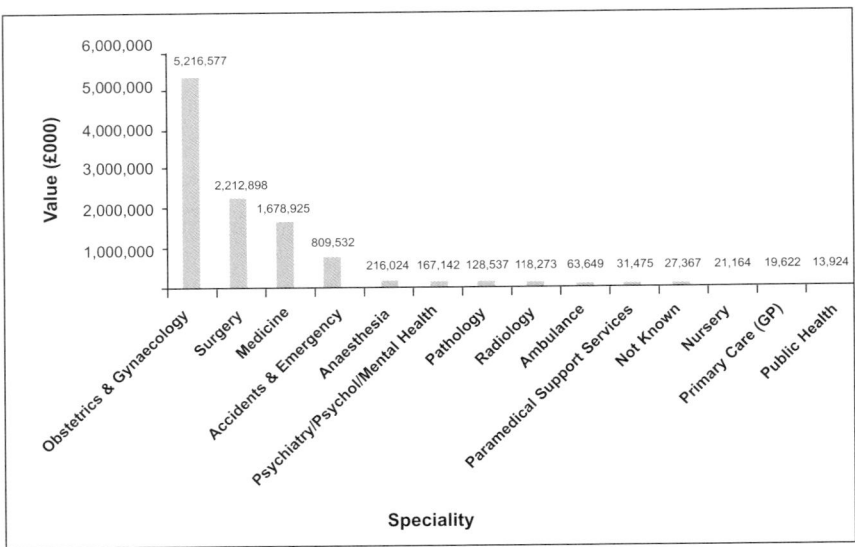

Figure 2: Total value of reported CNST claims by speciality as at 31/03/11(© NHSLA)[2]

Negligence claims involving obstetrics formed nearly two thirds of the damages claimed against the NHS in 2008/2009. They accounted for the biggest single category of claims (20%) made to the NHS Litigation Authority (NHSLA)[2] in that period, and were responsible for 60% of the total costs claimed.

In obstetrics, the most frequent reasons for suing a practitioner involves the mother and the child or fetus. Brain damage caused to the fetus constitutes the most common reason for the claim. Other problems in decreasing order are:

- perinatal death (31%)
- maternal operative injury (16%)
- perineal damage (15%)
- retained swab/instruments (5%)
- antenatal problem (5%).

In gynaecology, the problems directly correspond to the most frequent procedures performed. The commonest complication for claims is uterine perforation and ureteric damage. Other less common complications are:

- undiagnosed ectopic pregnancy
- problems with contraceptive
- sterilisation
- failed termination.

There are a host of other reasons, which comprise 20% of total litigation in gynaecology.

All health professionals, whether consultant, registrar, SHO, or midwife should be very careful and have clear understanding regarding the issues surrounding obtaining consent.

The management of patients in obstetrics and gynaecology is commonly medical and undertaken in outpatients or while the patient is conscious and awake. Therefore, it requires a slightly different approach in obtaining consent for these procedures (such as an outpatient day case procedure).

All in all a proper understanding of the whole process of consent, including the complications that may occur, are essential prerequisites of a successful and certainly a less litigious practice.

Part 1: Definition and Types of Consent

Consent literally means to give assent, to agree to the proposal of another.

Under common law, it has always been recognised that every person has the right to protect their bodily integrity against invasion by others. Medical treatment even of a minor nature should not proceed unless the doctor has first obtained the patient's consent. Failure to do so constitutes assault leading to civil claims, criminal prosecution and disciplinary procedures.

Consent may be implied or expressed (orally or in writing), and must be informed.

The nature of consent is difficult to define and is easier to characterise. Legal consent requires three elements to be present and a failure of any one element means that reaching consent has failed. These elements are thus interdependent rather than dependent; a combination of three separate but related elements.[3]

- **Voluntariness:** the willingness of one party to participate in a transaction; which means that the patient is competent enough to understand the procedure and its complications and is under no duress. Unless consent is given freely it is not valid in a court of law. The doctor taking consent should not put undue pressure on a patient to influence their decision. They should give full explanation to any questions including different treatment options, benefits and complications, without being biased. A woman should make her own informed choice voluntarily.
- **Capacity:** a sufficient degree of ability to understand the nature of the transaction (the patient is competent enough to make an independent choice regarding the procedure).
- **Knowledge:** a sufficient degree of information as to the nature of the transaction is disclosed to the participant in the transaction.

The most important goal of informed consent is that the patient has an opportunity to be an informed participant in her own healthcare decisions. It is generally accepted that complete informed consent includes a discussion of the following elements:
- the nature or type of the procedure
- reasonable alternatives to the proposed intervention, procedure or treatment
- the relevant risks, benefits, and uncertainties related to each alternative given

- clear assessment of the patient's understanding
- acceptance of the intervention by the patient.

Therefore, it follows that the patient has to be competent enough to take her own decision voluntarily regarding the procedure.

The woman must fully understand the nature, purpose and effect of proposed treatment before refusing it. If the treatment is carried out after refusal then the doctor can be charged with trespass. Consent is a defence to legal actions for battery, assault and false imprisonment, therefore proper documentation and record keeping is vital.

Informed Consent

Informed consent is defined as consent given by a patient to a surgical or medical procedure, or participation in a clinical study after the patient has achieved a full understanding of the relevant medical facts and the risks involved. The 'informed' element of consent depends upon the information given by the doctor and the understanding of their patient.

People need enough information so that they can decide whether to give consent or not. The information for informed consent requires all factors mentioned above including:
- procedure of the proposed treatment
- consequences of not having the treatment
- how a patient's life will be affected if they have or refuse the treatment.

Informed consent is a process by which a fully informed patient can participate in choices about her healthcare. The legal and ethical rights of the patient include the right to direct what happens to her body. The ethical and moral obligations of a physician direct him or her to involve the patient in her healthcare.

In summary, there has to be a detailed discussion about the procedure. The patient has to understand the discussion. She has to take a decision by her own will regarding the procedure and give assent to the procedure being undertaken.

Implied Consent

Implied consent means when a patient voluntarily accepts the procedure. A patient gives assent in certain, relatively routine procedures just by an action. For example, when a blood sample is drawn a patient usually rolls up her sleeve. Here, the core issue is that the procedure is relatively common. The patient understands the process as it is a common procedure and she need not be told in detail again. Furthermore, the action of rolling up of the sleeve in that particular context can only mean that the person is willing for blood sampling. It is presumed that the patient has sufficient knowledge of risk and benefits.

Expressed Consent

During consultation, after completion of the history, usually the health professional asks if it is all right to proceed further with the physical examination (e.g. for a chest, abdominal or a gynaecological examination). The patient makes an affirmative sound or action (by undressing). In this case, the physical examination is relatively common and the person expects it to be carried out at the end of history taking.

Usually patients understand in the single word 'examination' the whole process, as it is common knowledge. It is a usual practice to ask again if a more personal examination (per vaginal or rectal examination) is to be done as a part of the completion of the examination.

It is pertinent to note that even when taking a history, one should ask for permission before proceeding and reiterate if a sensitive part of the history has been reached, for example, sexual history, drug taking etc.[4]

Presumed Consent

The patient's consent is usually 'presumed' in emergency situations, e.g. when the patient is in an unconscious state or is incompetent. The patient's wishes and values may be quite different from the values of the physician. The principle of respect for the patient as a person obligates us to do our best and include their decision in the treatment plan. However, this is not always possible in emergency situations. The principle of beneficence may require the health professional to act on the patient's behalf when her life is at stake.

Interventions/Procedures Requiring Written Informed Consent

Health interventions such as surgery, anaesthesia, and other invasive procedures require a signed consent form. These signed forms should be the culmination of a dialogue required to foster the patient's informed participation in the clinical decision.

For a wide range of decisions, written consent is neither required nor needed, but some meaningful discussion and communication must take place. For instance, a woman contemplating screening for ovarian cancer should know the relevant argument for and against the screening test. The full implications of negative and positive screening should be discussed before undertaking the procedure.

It is generally considered that there are certain situations where written consent is a must and therefore procedures should not take place without it. The following are some of the situations when written consent is a must:

- the treatment or procedure is complex, or involves significant risks and/or side effects
- providing clinical care is not the primary purpose of the investigation or examination
- there may be significant consequences for the patient's employment, social or personal life
- the treatment is part of a research programme.

In other situations it is generally a clinician's decision whether consent should be oral or written. The consent must be recorded in a patient's case notes and where appropriate in a separate form. There are certain situations where it is a statutory requirement to obtain written consent from the patient (e.g. fertility treatment). In all such cases, local guidelines must be adhered to.

The written consent form should be examined to ensure adequate risks have been disclosed. It is good practice to be specific and detailed on the consent form. The doctor must explain about relevant issues and risks that the patient may be exposed to. Good documentation is necessary with legible writing and in simple language as this is very important in defending the case if there is a negligence claim.

Checklists can be important in obtaining informed consent, and should include:

1. Name of operation or proposed treatment
2. What the operation involves
3. Other treatment options or alternatives
4. Potential complications
5. Risks and benefits of treatment
6. Risks when treatment is not carried out
7. Special precaution post-operatively
8. Limitations of treatment
9. Success and failure rate of treatment.

Situations where Consent is not Required

Though consent is required in most of the situations, there are a few exceptions.[5] The examinations can continue even if the patient refuses to give consent. Examples for these are:

- medical examination of immigrants by the port or airport medical staff on entry into the United Kingdom
- psychiatric examination and/or treatment under the Mental Health Act 2007 and the Health Capacity Act 2005
- examination and/or treatment of a patient suffering from a notifiable disease (but a magistrate's order is a must)
- examination of dairymen or food handlers if there is a suspected outbreak of staphylococcus and salmonella
- external medical examination of new prisoners to exclude infectious disease
- external medical examination of members of the armed forces.

Part 2: Obtaining Consent

Becoming a patient can feel awkward. A patient might not have prior experience of the situation. Everyone feels some degree of powerlessness and vulnerability. To encourage voluntariness, the physician should make it clear to the patient that she is participating in a decision, not merely signing a form. The patient should see this as an invitation to participate in her healthcare decisions. Consequently, the discussion should be carried on in common terms. The patient's understanding should be assessed along the way.

Community consensus to some extent decides what is going to be the modus operandi for a particular scenario. For some minor issues it is not so relevant to go through all the steps of informed consent as the patient will be aware of the procedure and there is almost no chance of the procedure going wrong, for example, before taking a blood pressure measurement where the patient is supposed to be aware of the process, the usual approach is just to ask if it is all right to take the blood pressure measurement.

Informed consent is a process and should not be treated as a form to be signed only. Its fundamental aim is to ensure respect for people by enabling them to reach thoughtful consent for a voluntary act. The procedures used in obtaining informed consent should be designed to educate the subject in terms that they can understand. Information must be presented to enable patients to voluntarily decide whether or not to participate and have the procedure done. Therefore, informed consent language and its documentation (alternative risks, benefits, etc.) must be written in 'lay language'. Information used in the written document is the basis for consent and for future reference.

The document should be revised without any hesitation as soon as new information is available or the patient has expressed a desire to change a particular part of the consent. Any loophole must be plugged and the revisions made immediately.

Scientific jargon and legalese should be used as sparingly as possible, both when explaining to the patient and even later when the final document is prepared. Information given should be viewed as a teaching tool rather than a legal document. Explanations should include reasonable foreseeable harms, discomforts, inconvenience and risk associated with that particular operation or procedure. Any change or additional risk right up to the time of going for the operation should be recorded. If additional risks are identified during the course of consultation or before the operation (such as at an outpatient clinic or on a ward round) the consent process and documentation should be revised. This must be fully explained to the patient.

Informed consent should also include the benefits from the particular procedure being undertaken, and describe any alternative methods available which are comparable to the offered procedure. If the procedure is likely to affect psychological or social aspects then this should also be documented.

Informed consent should be taken in cases of procedures such as termination of pregnancy, where bereavement or guilt and sense of loss can be expected as a long-term complication. The language of consent must be carefully selected. It should not give the impression that the patient has agreed to blanket consent for any procedure, even if it is least likely to happen.

For consent to be valid the person must be an adult and give it voluntarily or where appropriate it is given by someone with parental responsibility (for a minor or young person or under 18).

For a person to have capacity, she must be able to comprehend and retain information material to the decision. It must be ensured that she understands the consequences of having or not having the intervention in question and be able to analyse and come to a decision. Patients may have the capacity to consent to some interventions but not others. All adults are presumed to have the capacity to do so unless there is some overriding reason. If there is any doubt about the capacity to give consent it should be noted in the patient's records.

There may be temporary factors that influence the assessment of a doctor as to the capacity of the patient, but the presence of these factors should not make one assume that the patient is incapable of giving consent.

There is a big difference between reasonableness and irrationality of the decision based on a patient's misperception of reality (but not on a set of different social, personal, cultural or religious value systems). Only in cases of a decision which is based on misperception of reality may a doctor question the patient's capacity. But, having a misperception is not in itself enough to make a person incapable of taking that decision.

There should not be an assumption that a patient who has a learning disability is unable to give consent. They are able to give consent in most cases after using special methods to communicate. The help of an appropriate therapist may be required.

In the case of a person who is unable to understand the English language it is imperative to make sure that an appropriate interpreter is available. The explanation should be given in the language the patient is most comfortable with. It is also a good practice to ensure the interpreter signs the form as well, thus documenting the use of an acceptable language.

Except in the case of an adult who has insufficient mental capacity, one should make sure that the decision is respected, even if it is deemed to be harmful or lethal, possibly even leading to the death of an unborn child in the case of a labouring mother.

There are two situations where a patient is considered unable to give informed consent:
1. Whereby because of unconsciousness a patient is unable to participate in her decision-making.
2. If the patient is deemed incompetent on the basis of a mental disorder, which makes her incapable of taking the right decisions.

Before obtaining consent a health professional has to be fully prepared. The process becomes easier as one gets more experienced with time. Thorough background work is essential before going about obtaining consent. Health professionals who are involved in taking consent should have all the information which they would like to give to the patient. The health professional must be ready to deal with the questions that may be put forward during the communication before obtaining the consent. Therefore, it is important to do prior preparation, use common sense and follow a structured methodology.

Standards for Consent

- Only a person who can perform the given procedure or has received specialist training in advising patients about a particular procedure (and has been assessed and found competent to do so) should obtain consent.
- A pre-registration house officer or any other grade should not obtain consent for any procedure which they are not supposed to perform. Their work should always be supervised and not be independent.

- As soon as the health professional meets the patient they should clearly introduce themselves, mentioning position or grade. They should make their ID card clearly visible to the patient, stating exactly why this conversation is taking place (i.e. they are there to obtain consent). A chaperone or a witness should be present if it is necessary and most importantly the health professional must check their local trust department policy or guidelines.
- They should clearly and in as simple words as possible go over the salient points of the patient's problems, and explain why the procedure was thought of as a possible alternative to management.
- They should outline the other modalities of treatment that are available, and then explain the pros and cons of each procedure in a language that she can understand.
- They should then outline all the steps of the procedure. It is a good idea to ask the patient to repeat what she has understood and assess if she is following the conversation or whether there is a need to go over the procedure again.
- They should then outline all the benefits that the procedure is supposed to bring about and the chances of success.
- Finally they should ask the patient if she has understood everything.

The Patient
Consent can only be obtained from the patient, parent or legal guardian. No adult, next of kin or otherwise should give consent to treatment on behalf of another adult.

Care should be taken in obtaining consent from a patient who has been pre-medicated. Certain medication and other substances such as alcohol may affect the patient's ability to give consent. In these circumstances the healthcare professional must first assess the patient's capacity to consent. If the patient does not have the capacity, then consent should not be obtained. Instead it should be delayed until the patient has been adjudged to be competent.

Details on the form that should be completed correctly and checked include:
- Name
- Date of birth
- Hospital number
- NHS or Insurance Number
- Name of Trust/Hospital

- Responsible healthcare professional (consultant responsible for patient's care)
- Special requirements
- Patient's signature, name and date in the correct place
- Doctor's signature, date, name and position in the correct place.

(A pre-printed label can be used for some of these details.) The patient should be offered a copy, which, if accepted will need to include the name of the proposed procedure or course of treatment, and a brief explanation if medical terms are not clear.

The treatment should be described on the consent form in words that the patient can understand. Abbreviations should not be used. The site and side of the operation must always be adequately specified. If there is doubt about the exact site this can be reflected in the wording, for example in ectopic pregnancy 'removal of affected tube' can be used.

The need for additional procedures should be mentioned in case of injury to the bowel, bladder, ureters, nerves, vessels, need for hysterectomy etc.

The statement of the healthcare professional includes:
- **The intended benefit:** Confirm the purpose and benefit from the operation. Medical terms should be explained if not clear.
- **Serious or frequently occurring risks:** Risks should be openly explained indicating the probability of each arising. There should be a mention of the likely seriousness, especially where the risk is >1%.

(*It should be indicated that the operation might not bring the desired benefit to the patient. There is a nebulous cut-off point which suggests that a doctor does not have to inform a patient of a risk if it is <1%. The question relates to how much risk should be told to the patient. The doctor must follow the standard established by the 'Bolam test' (a doctor is not negligent if he/she had acted in accordance with accepted practice by a responsible body) and 'Bolitho' cases (the opinion of an expert witness must be founded on logic and good sense).*)

- **All the extra procedures that may become necessary during the operation.**

- **Confirmation and documentation that the patient is willing for blood transfusion if necessary. If the patient refuses blood transfusion under any circumstance (e.g. is a Jehovah's Witness), a special form should be signed and the pre-signed health plan examined if necessary.**
- **Whether a leaflet/tape has been provided.**
- **Type of anaesthesia:** general or regional, etc.

Other Procedures:
- The extent of treatment must not exceed that defined either orally or on the consent form.
- If there is a possible additional procedure (e.g. emergency laparotomy in the course of laparoscopy, or oopherectomy while trying to conserve the ovaries, or hysterectomy during the course of caesarean section for placenta praevia), it should be stated clearly.
- Where there is a need to perform additional procedures beyond the scope of the consent these must be carried out if there is an immediate threat to the patient's life.

Signature:
- Name (print clearly).
- Title.
- Date.

Special Requirement:
- Statement of interpreter if appropriate.
- Statement of patient. This should include any procedures that the patient does not wish to be carried out.
- A witness should sign if the patient is unable to sign or indicate her consent on the form.

Confirmation of Consent:
If the patient has signed the form in advance, a health professional should confirm the consent when the patient is admitted for the procedure. This may require assessment of the validity of the indication (e.g. the baby is still breech before caesarean section), or surgery for utero-vaginal prolapse may need to be changed (e.g. vaginal hysterectomy instead of pelvic floor repair). Proper documentation of the discussion regarding indication, benefits, description of the procedure, risks and complications should be kept in the patient's notes. It should be documented in the case notes that the consent form has been signed.

Time Interval and Validity of Consent

If significant time has elapsed between the consent and the procedure then there is a possibility that clinical circumstances might have changed. The initial proposed treatment and the risk associated with the procedure may change. Consequently, reaffirmation of consent should be done by a clinician who understands and is familiar with the procedure, preferably the surgeon himself/herself.

Frequently Asked Questions by Patients

Questions may be about the treatment itself, for example:
- What is the main treatment option?
- What are the benefits of each of the options?
- What are the risks, if any, of each option?
- What is the success rate for different options – nationally, for this unit or for you (the surgeon)?
- Why do you think an operation (if suggested) is necessary?
- What are the risks if I decide to do nothing for the time being?
- How can I expect to feel after the procedure?
- When am I likely to be able to get back to work?

Questions may also be about how the treatment might affect the future state of health or lifestyle, for example:
- Will I need long-term care?
- Will my mobility be affected?
- Will I still be able to drive?
- Will it affect the kind of work I do?
- Will it affect my personal/sexual relationships?
- Will I be able to take part in my favourite sport/exercises?
- Will I be able to follow my usual diet?

The Appropriate Time to Question a Patient's Ability to Participate in Decision-Making

In most cases it is clear whether or not patients are competent to make their own decisions. Occasionally patients are under an unusual amount of stress during illness and can experience anxiety, fear and depression. This should not necessarily preclude them from participating in their own care. However, precautions should be taken to ensure the patient does have the capacity to make proper decisions.

It is important to assess the patient's ability to:
- understand her situation
- understand the risks associated with the decision at hand
- communicate a decision based on that understanding.

When this is unclear, a psychiatric consultation can be helpful. Refusal of treatment does not in itself mean the patient is incompetent. Patients who are competent have the right to refuse treatment (even those treatments that may be life-saving). However, treatment refusal may encourage the health practitioner to pursue further the patient's beliefs and understanding about the decision.

Patient Whose Decision-Making Capacity Varies from Day-to-Day

Patients can move in and out of a coherent state as their medications or underlying processes ebb and flow. An attempt should be made to ensure that the patient is in a lucid state before consent is taken and this may involve medical help. It is a good idea to confirm the consent in subsequent lucid states to ensure a consistency of belief but it also gives a good indication about the state of the patient. If doubts persist or if the patient changes her views regularly, it is a good idea to withhold treatment and seek a psychiatric consultation.

Important Issues and the Dynamics of Consent

First of all, each situation has its own pitfalls and each person has their own way of reacting to a given situation. This should always guide the healthcare practitioner in deciding how they should go about getting fully informed consent. Furthermore, a patient is always worried about misinformation or lack of information rather than excessive information. It is important to try to gather as much information about the patient as possible before starting the interview. One should also know as much as possible about the disease and/or the procedure that is in focus. One should never volunteer anything that carries even the vaguest traces of doubt in a patient's mind. Asking the patient about her special concerns is a must as this often brings out something that has been glossed over and deemed to be considered too much information by the medical staff, but in actual fact is very important to the patient.

Nowadays a patient has remarkably good access to information through the Internet and books. Therefore it is important to know their level of understanding about the subject. Their views and understanding should be discussed thoroughly rather than discarded.

Health professionals should be aware of a patient's special religious and cultural concerns (rather than just 'trying' to understand them). A closure at the end with enough feedback from the person that enables us to be confident about her being informed is a must. Health professionals must be aware of the recent rulings and changes in the laws governing medico-legal issues as it can be vary between regions.

The golden rule which must always be remembered is that any doubts must be passed onto the person higher in the chain of responsibility (e.g. the consultant).

The whole process of consent becomes an interesting one, especially if one sees a new junior doctor taking consent from a worried patient. It is an interactive process, where both the consentee and consenter have an active role to play. The whole process is a result of this interplay.

One of the common mistakes is to assume that the patient is a task and not a person. The patient is not just a recording machine, but is able to understand the information that has been provided to her. She will assimilate the information and store it according to her understanding of the situation. There are few obvious variables in the equation, such as the patient's intelligence, cultural background, educational level and her priority of importance of the issues involved. In addition the person obtaining consent has to have a thorough knowledge of the issues involved. Sometimes it can be a lengthy and boring process to endure, the success of which depends on the practitioner's level of experience in dealing with patients, and this can be very variable. To begin with the process of consent taking may be a lot more difficult, but it becomes refined and polished with every additional patient.

Different circumstances warrant different strategies. In certain situations one should be sure that a person is capable of giving informed consent.[6] Sometimes post-surgery in the ITU setting a patient is not in a position to give consent, either due to the post-anaesthetic state or psychosis. Therefore, care should be taken not to make the mistake of obtaining consent in a situation where the patient has no understanding of what is being proposed.

Patients whose First Language is other than English

It is important that the patient whose first language is not English should be communicated appropriately with through the interpreter. If there is a staff member/health professional who can speak the same language, they should act as an interpreter.

Usually it is not advisable for children in the family to be the interpreter. There should be a list of the interpreters available in emergency situations (bleep or telephone number). For routine appointments an interpreter should be organised by prior notice. A patient should not be at a disadvantage due to the language barrier.

It is important to make sure conversation regarding the treatment options is understood by the patient and has not been interpreted in another way before taking any kind of consent (even if it only includes physical examination).

Part 3: The Law and Consent

How much Information is Considered Adequate?

It is always difficult for anyone to decide when enough information has been given to a patient. It is a matter of clinical judgement and varies with the amount of experience and expertise of the surgeon concerned. It also depends upon the patient's ability to understand and her importance in decision-making in certain situations. Therefore it can be difficult to know whether enough discussion has taken place about a certain situation or procedure.

The GMC has provided some guidelines[7] on how much information is required or sufficient regarding the type of risk factors, as there is always some confusion. Currently required are:
- the purpose of the investigation and treatment
- diagnosis, differential diagnosis
- the options and their advantages and disadvantages, successes and failures
- all side effects
- the percentage of risk for the procedure including the personal data of success rate for that particular surgeon performing the surgery.

If sufficient information is not provided in a form the patient understands then it can be challenged by the Human Rights Act.

Most of the literature and law in this area suggests one of the following three approaches:

Reasonable physician standard
What would a typical physician say about the intervention?
This standard allows the physician to determine what information is appropriate to disclose. Most research in this area shows that the typical physician tells the patient very little. This standard is also generally considered inconsistent with the goals of informed consent as the focus is on the physician rather than on the patient's need to know.

Reasonable patient standard
What would the average patient need to know in order to be an informed participant in the decision?
This standard focuses on considering what a patient would need to know in order to understand the decision at hand. The question of how much information is enough is one that meets both the professional obligation to provide the best care, and respects the patient as a person with the right to be involved in healthcare decisions.

Subjective standard

What would this patient need to know and understand in order to make an informed decision?

This standard is the most challenging to incorporate into practice since it requires tailoring information to each patient as a different individual according to their need.

The amount of information that has to be disclosed to the patients and relatives remains a topic of intense legal and ethical debate. Many patients would like to know the potential problems in great details while others would like only the minimum of information.

A careful balance is required to ensure that patients who are not willing to know precise details as it may cause them distress, have sufficient knowledge to make an informed choice.

Sometimes the patient requests a doctor to make the decision on their behalf. In such cases it is the duty of the health professional to explain to the patient the options open to them and then detail the procedure. If a patient refuses to know the details of the diagnosis or treatment involved, the doctor still must provide basic information about the treatment, which will depend on individual circumstances. In a difficult situation where the risk is anticipated to be high then written documentation should be taken from the patient showing their unwillingness to receive detailed information.

The information imparted can also vary according to the relevance given to a particular patient of the possibility of increased complications related to the particular procedure. For instance, before a hysterectomy for menstrual problems in a 30 year old obese patient, more emphasis may be given to the risk of venous thromboembolic disease than to excessive details about potential bowel injury (since she is at an increased risk of developing DVT rather than an increased risk of bowel injury). On the other hand, it is important to discuss the possibilities of bowel injury in detail to women going for the same operation who have an endometrial carcinoma, or have had multiple abdominal incisions.

Informed consent is a technical term to some extent and has different meanings to different people. For a lawyer it relates to the patient-oriented consent that is the norm in USA.[8] In England the situation is somewhere between the patient and the physician-driven standard. Hence, it is important to note at this point that the mainstay of decisions in court is not whether a particular thing was said or not, but whether it would have been said if it was considered part of a normal medical practice.

The commonly followed and recognised methodology of decisions in English law is from the 'Bolam test'.[9] Since 1957 the Bolam test has been the benchmark by which professional negligence has been assessed. It is based on the direction to the jury of High Court Judge, McNair J, in Bolam v. Friern Hospital Management Committee.

> "A doctor is not guilty of negligence if he has acted in accordance with a practice accepted as proper by a responsible body of medical men skilled in that particular art. Putting it another way round, a doctor is not negligent if he is acting in accordance with such a practice, merely because there is a body of opinion that takes a contrary view." [9]

The Bolam test requires the doctor to act in accordance with a standard accepted as proper by a responsible body of medical opinion. It is in many ways a subjective test. The guidelines that are emerging require obtaining patient-oriented consent.[10] The issue about how much information should be provided before a patient gives consent has been considered by the Court of Appeal. When deciding how much information to provide to a patient a doctor must take into account all the relevant circumstances mentioned before.

The issue of consent has assumed a significant place in the medical negligence debate in recent years, especially in claims of female sterilisation. Some would argue that the minimum information disclosed should be the 'prudent patient' standard (i.e. what the patient thinks she should be told). Whilst others argue that it should be the professional standard (i.e. what the doctor thinks the patient should be told). The patient should be informed as fully as possible about the nature and consequences of treatment and whether an alternative is available, in a manner that the patient comprehends.

Lord Woolf indicated that it is for the court and not for the medical professions to decide on the appropriate standard as to what should be disclosed to the patient about a particular treatment.[11] Normally the legal duty of the doctor is to advise the patient about any significant risk which may affect the judgement of a reasonable patient in making a decision about a treatment. Where risk is 1–2% per 1000 it is not considered a significant risk.

If the risk is serious, no matter how rare the occurrence is, the patient should be informed. Usually these uncommon serious complications are presented as part of a written documentation given to the patient. In some cases it can be a possible reason for a change of decision by the patient, and then it is best discussed with the patient in person.

How much Information is needed in an Emergency Situation?

In an emergency a doctor is not required to take consent if the patient is unable to do so and a delay in treatment may result in her death or in a serious adverse effect. Furthermore, if time is of the essence, detailed informed consent need not be taken if the salient points are covered and the patient agrees to them.

The treatment should only be of such a nature that it is sufficient to save the patient's life and/or prevent deterioration in her condition. Even in an emergency, advance directives should be respected as soon as they are brought to attention. The patient still has a right to be told all that has taken place when she was unable to participate in her decision making. As soon as she is in a state to understand it should be explained to her.

Medical Negligence

In recent years there has been a marked increase in litigation claims and financial awards. The number of claims made does not always proceed to an action of medical negligence in the UK. There are practical difficulties in linking the injury to the plaintiff to medical treatment. Also, in medical negligence cases the courts still effectively allow the standard of care to be defined by the medical profession itself.

The seminal legal cases are those of Hunter v. Hanley in Scotland [Hunter v. Hanley 1955 SC 200] and the English case of Bolam [Bolam v. Friern Hospital Management Committee [1957] 2 All ER 118, [1957] 1 WLR 582], both of which define the essence of medical negligence. The Bolam dictum is applicable not only to diagnosis and treatment but also to the giving of information.

If a patient suffers harm as a result of treatment in a hospital she may bring action for damages against the hospital. Vicarious liability means that the employing NHS trust is liable for any errors made by the doctor in the course of his or her employment.

For an action of medical negligence to succeed the patient must be able to show three things:

1. The doctor owed the patient a duty of care.
2. The doctor was in breach of that duty (i.e. failed to provide care of an adequate standard).
3. The patient suffered harm as a consequence of that breach.

The burden of proof lies with the patient pursuing a claim of negligence. It is for the patient to show that, on the balance of probabilities, the doctor failed to meet the standard of care expected.

Confidentiality

The requirement to protect patient confidentiality has long been included in the ethical code of healthcare professionals (e.g. the Hippocratic Oath). Protecting patient confidentiality may give rise to some moral and legal dilemmas (e.g. young girls requesting contraception, HIV testing in pregnancy).

There are exceptions to the confidentiality rule. These include emergency situations, if the health or safety of the others is placed at serious risk, or if it is felt to be in the patient's best interests for confidentiality to be breached. Patients should always be told before confidentiality is breached.[12]

From January 2005, staff, patients, and members of the public have had a legal right to request any piece of recorded information that is kept by or on behalf of public authorities.[13] The request can be made retrospectively dating back many years. This is intended to promote a culture of openness and accountability amongst public sector bodies. This facilitates better understanding of how public authorities carry out their duties, the mechanism of decision-making and how public money is spent. However, this Act does not change existing data protection legislation or Caldicott Guidelines.

The Data Protection Act 1998[14] protects personal privacy and encourages good practice in the handling of personal information about an individual's own health and financial records. This Act applies to all bodies that process personal information, not only to public authorities. There can be a breach of confidentiality only when information was provided which was not previously available to a third party. Usually to inform the husband that his wife is pregnant is not considered to be a breach of confidentiality. But telling him that she is contemplating a termination of pregnancy is considered to be a breach of confidentiality. The patient might not like to disclose this information and to do so is her personal choice. If a patient gives specific instructions that someone is not to be informed about their condition then this must be respected. Such instructions should be recorded in the notes and passed on to all staff involved in the patient's care.

It is not proper to disclose the information to someone who is not currently involved in the care of the patient, apart from her previous physician. Anyone who is not involved in the care of the patient (including managers and administrators) should only have access to the unidentifiable data.

If the person constitutes an occupational health risk then it is the duty of the doctor to release only the relevant part of the medical data to the employers. In cases of abuse of the elderly, children or mentally incompetent individuals, the doctor is duty bound to report the incident and breach confidentiality.

Genetic Information

The principle of confidentiality applies to genetic information as well. In cases where the information is of importance to the chances of a child being born with an anomaly, it remains the duty of the physician to safeguard the confidentiality. In cases of this information being vital to the mental well-being of other family members, the doctor must weigh the pros and cons very carefully. There should be discussion between the doctor and the patient if any breach of confidentiality is considered. An attempt to persuade the patient to agree to voluntary disclosure of information should be encouraged.

Risk Management including Risk of Litigation

Appropriate management is essential in avoiding litigation and minimising the cost. Careful decision-making, explanation of possible complications and complete documentation are the best defence. Informed consent should include every eventuality including a discussion of complications, like bowel obstruction, bladder injury in pelvic surgery.

All records should be kept and written legibly. If the record is incomplete an additional record should be kept, also dated and signed.

Each entry in a patient's notes should be made in black ink and include the date and time of the consultation and signature of the practitioner. The name, grade and contact number for the practitioner should be written in capital letters beneath each entry. Original records should not be amended. If changes have to be made they should be clearly recorded separately with the date and time of the amendment as well as the name and signature of the person doing it.

An incident or risk management form should be filled in immediately if there is a possibility of a complaint regarding the care provided. If there is any doubt the Defence Union should be contacted for advice regarding the course of action and possible scenarios.

If a patient develops a complication and the healthcare provider is aware of the problem, an honest explanation should be given to the patient without any cover up. All facts should be collected before talking to the patient. Where the patient is unable to discuss or understand the information given, a next of kin should be present or informed.

The facts should be given to the patient or relative by the most senior doctor available (consultant). Often patients or their relatives feel an extra sense of being wronged if a junior doctor is asked to convey the 'bad news'. An empathetic attitude is very important and practitioners should not be afraid or hesitant to apologise. Every attempt should be made to win the patient's confidence.

If complications arise they should be taken seriously. Appropriate management should be initiated and correct and full information given to the patient and relatives. Advice from senior colleagues and specialists should be sought at an early stage.

Clinical governance is becoming an increasingly important part of healthcare. It is essential that mistakes are acknowledged and lessons learned to prevent avoidable errors occurring again. Even if it is felt that somebody else has made an error, it is unwise to criticise another healthcare professional in front of patients, particularly if all the facts are not yet known. However, if a mistake has been made it is good practice to admit it and apologise to the patient immediately. This does not imply negligence. Indeed, failure to disclose the error is often equated with incompetence. Admission of errors to patients or fellow colleagues is sometimes difficult. In simple words, nobody is perfect, and not everybody possesses a retrospectoscope by which complications can be predicted.

In the present culture, NHS and insurance agencies prefer to settle out of court to minimise costs. With the cost of a court case generally much more than the cost of settlement in most cases, the employer is not necessarily willing to go to court to clear the name of the practitioner. So it is very important that one takes all necessary care while practising medicine.

Legal Consequences of Lack of Consent

A procedure carried out on a patient without the patient's consent is prima facie an infringement of that patient's rights and may give rise to remedies in criminal and civil law.

Civil remedies arising from lack of consent give rise to actions in tort (a civil wrong). There are two actions in tort which are relevant: battery and negligence. Battery is the unlawful infliction of force upon another person; it is a form of trespass to the person.

A caesarean section (CS) performed without consent to save the life of a fetus could go to the court for battery. If the case was proven, the medical practitioner who performed the CS could end up in prison. The only situation in which a CS can be performed without consent is if the mother is unconscious and delivery of the child would save the mother's life, or if the mother is deemed incompetent to give consent.

The definition of incompetence is defined within the Mental Health Act 2007.[15] It is essential that more than one practitioner determines whether a patient is competent or incompetent in order that the charge of battery or assault cannot be brought.

Consent where there is a Feto-Maternal Conflict

Competent adult patients are entitled to refuse treatment, even where it would clearly benefit their health. The only exception to this rule is where the treatment is for a mental disorder and the patient is detained under the Mental Health Act 2007. Therefore, a competent pregnant woman may refuse any treatment, even if this would be detrimental to the fetus.

Recent cases of court authorised CS have highlighted the difficulties faced by doctors when a pregnant woman refuses to accept treatment that is thought by medical staff to be in the best interests of either herself or her baby.[16] Judgements from the High Court, which sanctioned the performance of CS against the mother's wishes, received strong criticism for two main reasons. They contradict the generally held principle of the right to self-determination (autonomy). Many legal cases have demonstrated that, provided a patient has sufficient mental capability to understand the treatment options available, they have the right to refuse treatment even if it endangers their own life.

It has been established in both the civil and criminal law that the fetus is not a person with legal rights and, as such, the courts do not have the power to protect the fetus.

The Court of Appeal subsequently reviewed these cases and concluded that it is unlawful to perform a CS against a woman's wishes if she is mentally competent. It is recommended that problem cases should be identified and brought before the courts early if it is to be an elective procedure. There should be evidence, preferably from a psychiatrist, as to the woman's background and her mental capacity, and she should be legally represented in court. Doctors are under a duty to respect an advanced directive (i.e. expressed in advance of the emergency) from a competent patient refusing consent (e.g. one cannot perform a CS against the patient's wishes if an advanced directive has been given against this).

Part 4: Consent in Special Circumstances

Consent for Children and Young Individuals

The legal requirements concerning consent and the refusal of treatment for someone under the age of 18 is different to that of an adult. A child becomes competent from the day he or she turns 16. From that point onwards the person can give both oral and written consent for themselves.

Under the age of 16, a child can be presumed to be competent for a condition where they fully understand what is proposed. In cases where they cannot it is important to involve the person with parental responsibility. In the UK, 'children' refers to those aged below 16 and 'young people' are defined as those aged 16–17.[17]

The law relating to children and young people is complex and differs across the UK. Therefore all doctors who work with this population must have clear understanding of the law where they practice.[18]

Young people are presumed to be capable of making decisions and consenting to their own health and medical treatment. This might involve surgical procedure or anaesthetics. It is a very similar process to the adults' (consent is only valid if it is voluntary and given after full and appropriate information, only by the person capable of doing that particular intervention).

It is not legally necessary for the parents or guardian to give consent on their behalf or in addition. However, unlike with adults, their decision can be overridden by the court or the parents (those with parental responsibility/guardian) if it is beneficial for their health.

It is good practice to involve parents/guardian in the decision-making process if a young person wishes. It should not be done against their wishes if they do not want the information to be shared and they understand the consequences.

Children under 16 – the Concept of Gillick Competence

A young person (aged 16 or 17 years) or a child under 16 who is Gillick competent can consent to treatment in accordance with Section 8 of the Family Law Reform Act of 1969. Gillick competence[18] relates to the particular condition and particular treatment for a particular child. A doctor can decide whether a child is Gillick competent or not where the court is reluctant to do so. If a situation is faced with a competent child or young person who refuses to consent to treatment, then it is prudent to obtain a court declaration to determine whether it is lawful to treat the child.

According to English law, additional consent by a person with parental responsibility is not required if the child is Gillick competent and able to give consent voluntary. It is important to make sure that they receive appropriate information and their decision has not been influenced by their parents or sexual partner.

However, refusal for treatment could be overruled if it would in all probability lead to the death of the child/young person or to severe permanent injury. There might be emergency situations where a young person and the person of parental responsibility refuse to consent to treatment which is in the best interest of the young person. In such cases the court takes the decision in favour of the preservation of life.

In the case of a child (less than 16 years of age and not Gillick competent), consent can be given on their behalf by any one person with parental responsibility or by the court. It is a good practice to involve the child as much as possible in the decision-making even if they lack capacity. That the consent must be exercised according to the 'welfare principle' (i.e. the child's 'welfare') or 'best interests' is most important.

The court's decision should be requested in some important decisions, such as sterilisation and where there is a disagreement regarding whether the procedure is in the best interest of the child. The court has the power to refuse the consent given by a person with parental responsibility. They must have the capacity (and if less than 18, should be Gillick competent themselves).

The law in relation to parental responsibility has recently been revised. For a child whose birth was registered from 15 April 2002 in Northern Ireland, 1 December 2003 in England and Wales and 4 May 2006 in Scotland, both of the child's parents have parental responsibility if they are registered on the child's birth certificate.

Persons who may have Parental Responsibility

UK

These include (according to The Children Act 1989):
- the child's mother (a mother always has parental responsibility for her child)
- the child's father, if he was married to the mother at the time of birth
- the child's legally appointed guardian
- a person whose favour the court has made a residence order concerning the child.

Unmarried fathers can acquire parental responsibility as shown:
- For children born before 1 December 2003 if they
  - marry the mother of their child or obtain a parental responsibility order from the court or register a parental responsibility agreement with the court
- For children born after 1 December 2003 if they
  - register the child's birth jointly with the mother at the time of birth
  - re-register the birth if they are the natural father
  - marry the mother of their child
  - obtain a parental responsibility order from the court or register with the court.

Anyone who does not meet the above criteria is not responsible for consent, and this applies to foster, step and grandparents or other relatives. For a ward of court, the court must approve all the treatments (or there should be a mention of routine treatments that may be necessary). It is reasonable to make sure that the patient is involved even though they cannot consent for themselves.

Children younger than 16 may also give consent, especially if they are able to fully understand the implications of the proposed procedure. If a competent child consents to treatment or a procedure, a parent cannot override that. Health professionals should respect a decision taken by the young person, which is beneficial for the child. Where the child refuses the treatment, legally it is possible for the parent to give consent (although this is a rare situation).

USA

Law for minors (age 12 and older) to consent for certain conditions in the

USA (such as sexual and reproductive healthcare, mental health services and alcohol and drug abuse treatment) has developed dramatically over the past 30 years. The change was due to the realization that many minors would not avail an important service if there is parental involvement. Law in every state is different. However, the majority permits all or some minors to obtain contraceptives, and STI services without parental involvement. In contrast parental involvement is required in most states if a minor requires an abortion.

Some states allow only certain groups of minors (who are married, pregnant or already parents) to consent. In those states where there is no law, doctors provide the care without parental consent, to those who they deem mature.

Contraceptive Services: 26 states and the District of Columbia allow all minors to consent, 20 allow only certain categories and 4 have no relevant policy or case law.

STI Services: All states and the District of Columbia allow all minors to consent and it is not necessary to inform parents if it is not in the best interest of the minor.

Adoption: 28 states and the District of Columbia allow all minor parents to choose to place their child for adoption. In addition, 5 states require the involvement of a parent and 5 states require the involvement of legal counsel. The remaining 12 states have no relevant policy or case law.

Medical Care for a Child: 30 states and the District of Columbia allow all minors' parents to consent to medical care for their child. The remaining 20 states have no relevant explicit policy or case law.

Abortion: 2 states and the District of Columbia explicitly allow all minors to consent to abortion services. 20 states require that at least one parent's consent, 12 states require prior notification of at least one parent, 4 require both notification and consent from a parent, and 6 additional states have parental involvement laws that are temporarily or permanently enjoined. 6 states have no relevant policy or case law.

Sexual Health and Contraception

The new guidance highlights for the first time that where a person under the age of 16 makes a request for contraception, doctors and other health professionals should establish a rapport with the young person. They should give the young person the time and support needed to make an informed choice.[19]

They should discuss:
- The emotional and physical implications of sexual activity, including the risks of pregnancy and sexually transmitted infections.
- Whether the relationship is mutually agreed, coercive or abusive.
- The benefits of informing their GP and encouraging discussion with a parent or carer. Any refusal should be respected.
- In the case of abortion, where the young woman is competent to consent but cannot be persuaded to involve a parent, every effort should be made to help them find another adult to provide support (for example another family member or specialist youth worker).

The duty of confidentiality is not absolute where a health professional believes that there is a risk to the health, safety or welfare of a young person or others, which is so serious as to outweigh the young person's right to privacy. They should follow agreed child protection protocols. In these circumstances, the overriding objective must be to safeguard the young person.

Additionally, it is considered good practice for doctors and other health professionals to follow the criteria outlined by Lord Fraser (in 1985 in the House of Lords' ruling in the case of Victoria Gillick v. West Norfolk and Wisbech Health Authority and Department of Health and Social Security).

These are commonly known as the Fraser Guidelines, which specifically relate to contraception but do apply to other treatments as well, including abortion in England and Wales:[20]
- the young person understands the health professional's advice and has sufficient maturity to understand what is involved
- the health professional cannot persuade the young person to inform her parent or allow the doctor to inform the parents that she is seeking contraceptive advice
- the young person is very likely to begin or continue having intercourse with or without contraceptives
- without contraception the young person's physical or mental health will suffer
- it is in the best interest of the young person to give advice and treatment or both, with or without parental consent.

In the best interests of the young person, the health professional should give contraceptive advice, treatment or both without parental consent (where physical or mental health or both are likely to suffer).

In Scotland, the Age of Legal Capacity Act (1991) states that "a person under the age of 16 years shall have legal capacity to consent on their own behalf to any surgical, medical or dental procedure or treatment." The person must have understanding of the nature and possible consequences in the opinion of a qualified medical practitioner.

Consent for Abortion

Consent from a girl under 16 years depends on the maturity and understanding of an individual. If the doctor is satisfied that the girl understands the nature and possible complications of the procedure, issues involved and refuses to involve her parents, then the Fraser guidance may be used. If the doctor believes that an abortion is in the best interest of the girl then it can be carried out.

Prisoners as Patients

Though prisoners do not have the right to choose their doctors, they are able to give consent like any other individual. The guideline for obtaining consent is the same as for any other person. If the prisoner is violent or agitated, the guideline for mentally incompetent persons is to be followed.

Mentally Incompetent

The Mental Capacity Act
The Mental Capacity Act 2005[22] came fully into force in England and Wales on 1 October 2007 and helps ensure patients who lack capacity participate as much as possible in decision-making about their health and care.

The main implications are:
  • how to judge capacity
  • lasting powers of attorney
  • on advance decisions.

The principle of the Mental Capacity Act applies to all health professionals working with and caring for a person who lacks capacity. It is an offence by someone with responsibility of care and decision-making power to ill-treat or wilfully neglect a person who lacks capacity. Therefore any decision made on their behalf has to be in their best interest by considering all the relevant circumstances.

The Act rules that healthcare professionals **must:**
- decide whether the person is likely to regain capacity and if so whether the decision can wait
- involve the person in the decision-making that is being made on their behalf
- consider the person's past and present wishes, especially if they are written down
- look at any beliefs and values (e.g. religious, cultural or moral) that would be likely to influence the decision and other relevant factors
- consult other people (previously named, anyone engaging in caring for or interested in the person's welfare, any attorney appointed under a Lasting Power of Attorney (LPA) and deputy appointed by the Court of Protection) as appropriate to make sure a decision taken is in the best interests of the person.

Where there is no one appropriate other than healthcare professionals, then an Independent Mental Capacity Advocate should be instructed for decisions about serious medical treatment if the decision is regarding whether the withdrawal of life-sustaining treatment should be in the best interest of the person.

The Mental Capacity Act enables a person aged 18 or over to appoint an attorney to look after their health and welfare decisions.

Under a personal welfare, people with LPA are also able to make decisions that are as valid as those made by the person themselves. The LPA must be registered with the Office of the Public Guardian and meet the criteria before it can be used. LPA must specify whether or not the attorney has the authority to make decisions about life-sustaining treatment.

Healthcare practitioners directly involved in the care or treatment should not agree to act as an attorney unless they are the only close relative. Parents, relatives or healthcare team members cannot give consent on behalf of the patient. If the refusal was given when the patient was competent or in the period of remission in case of a mental disorder, the refusal is generally considered to be valid. If there is a dispute between the attorney and a doctor that cannot be resolved, it may have to be referred to the Court of Protection.

Independent Mental Capacity Advocates (IMCA)

The Mental Capacity Act (April 2007 in England and since October 2007 in Wales), introduced a duty on NHS bodies to instruct an IMCA in serious medical treatment decisions. IMCAs are not decision-makers, but support, represent and ensure that decision-making for people who lack capacity is done appropriately and in accordance with the Mental Capacity Act.

The duties of an IMCA are to:
- support and represent a patient's views and interests to the decision-maker
- obtain and evaluate information from both parties by interviews or reviewing the case notes
- identify alternative courses of action and obtain a further medical opinion if required and prepare a report.

Referral to Court

Referral to the court is made before a procedure is undertaken in the following situations:
- decisions about the proposed withholding or withdrawal of ANH from patients in a permanent vegetative state
- cases involving organ, bone marrow or peripheral blood stem cell donation
- cases involving proposed non-therapeutic sterilisation (e.g. for contraceptive purposes)
- all other cases where there is a dispute about whether a particular treatment will be in a person's best interests.

Sterilisation which is incidental to the management of the detrimental effects of menstruation and abortion need not automatically be referred to the court if there is no doubt that this is the most appropriate action.

It is good practice to involve a multidisciplinary team in the decision-making process, including a consultant in the psychiatry of learning disability and the patient's family. Proper documentation should be kept of their involvement. Less invasive or reversible options should always be considered before permanent sterilisation. For the management of menstrual problems, hysterectomies should be undertaken only after great care has been taken in determining the best interests of the woman.

It is a good idea to delay treatment if there is a scope for improvement and the procedure required is not urgent. The guiding principle should always be: best interest of the patient and not best medical interest.

There are certain situations where it is appropriate to seek a ruling from the court before a procedure is undertaken:
- sterilisation for contraceptive purposes
- donation of regenerative tissue such as bone marrow
- withdrawal of nutrition and hydration from a patient in a persistent vegetative state
- where there is a doubt as to the patient's capacity or best interests.

The courts have the opinion that neither sterilisation that is part of the management of menstrual disorder nor abortion need automatically be referred to court. If there is a concern about the best interest then possibly it should be done. In a patient with severe learning disabilities it is important to involve a consultant psychiatrist in the decision-making process, and to document their involvement. Less invasive or reversible options should always be considered first.[23]

Post-Mortem Examination

Policies on consent for post-mortem examination and tissue retention are regulated by the Human Tissue (HT) Act 2004.[24] Post-mortem is a medical examination of a dead body. Usually the coroner requests a post-mortem examination (it can be requested by the hospital or a close relative).

The next of kin must give detailed written consent to the post-mortem examination; it could be either for a full or limited examination. The named next of kin may not be the person in the highest ranking qualifying relationship under the HT Act; therefore it is important to find the appropriate person. Ranking of relationships is done in order of importance, which is as follows:

1. Spouse or partner
2. Parent or child
3. Brother or sister
4. Grandparent or grandchild
5. Child of a brother or sister
6. Stepfather or stepmother
7. Half-brother or half-sister
8. Longstanding friend.

Where consent from a person in a qualifying relationship cannot be obtained, the post-mortem examination cannot proceed.

The first step of a post-mortem examination is to obtain consent. If a post-mortem is ordered by a coroner, consent or agreement of next of kin is not required as it must take place by law.

If a post-mortem is requested by a hospital, written consent from the nominated representative or the next of kin is required. It is possible that the patient may have given their consent before death.

In order to comply with the HT Act, codes of practice and HTA standards, Designated Individuals (DI) are required to assure themselves that appropriate consent is obtained by properly trained practitioners for hospital post-mortem examinations.

As part of a post-mortem carried out by a hospital, the pathologist may wish to take samples of tissue or remove organs for further study and research. This can only be done if the next of kin gives consent for continued storage or use of tissue once the coroner's purposes are complete.

Use of Tissues and Organs

The use of the tissues of a patient for purposes other than diagnostic (which are covered in the consent for surgery) requires separate and specific consent.

Any use of the tissues in research or education should be done after the patient has given consent. Use of fetal tissue in transplantation or research should only take place after consent and without anyone benefiting financially from it. Informed consent is required from the donor or the next of kin if the donor has died.

Research should only go ahead if the potential benefits outweigh any risks to the donors. Donations should be viewed as gifts without financial gain, treated with respect and must be approved by an appropriately constituted research ethics committee.[25]

Consent for Vaginal Examination for Gynaecological Procedures

Due to the increasing incidence of allegation of assaults by patients against doctors, especially where intimate bodily examinations are involved, it is strongly recommended that chaperones should be present when examining a patient of the opposite sex. They often help in reassuring the patient as well as minimise the risk of misinterpretation if complaints occur in future.[26, 27, 28, 29] Chaperones also act as an impartial observer, and offer reassurance if a woman shows signs of distress or discomfort during the examination.

Intimate examination relates to genital (including speculum) or rectal examination and palpation of breasts. It is important to maintain a professional boundary as these examinations can be embarrassing and sometimes distressing for a woman.

Proper explanation should be given regarding the procedure and should be stopped if a woman objects to it. Unnecessary remarks or comments should not be made during the examination.

If a woman is anaesthetised, written consent should be taken beforehand (in the case of a medical student valid consent is necessary).

The most common cause of patient complaints is a failure on the patient's part to understand what the doctor was doing in the process of diagnosing and treating them. Ideally the name of the chaperone should be documented in the notes.

It is important that:
- the examination is genuinely needed and discussed with the patient
- the healthcare practitioner explains precisely what the purpose of the examination is and gives the patient an opportunity to ask questions
- if a chaperone is not available then the examination should be done by someone of the same sex, otherwise the patient should be asked to come back according to the availability of a chaperone
- consent should be recorded in the notes if the patient is anaesthetised and consent must be obtained before anaesthetisation (usually in writing)
- each stage of the examination should be explained and preparation taken to stop the examination if the patient asks to do so
- discussion is relevant and unnecessary personal comments should be avoided
- the patient is given privacy to undress and dress (use drapes to maintain the patient's dignity and do not assist the patient in removing clothing unless it has been clarified that assistance is required)

- the examination should not be carried out if management does not change
- if the patient does not speak English, an interpreter should be present
- in the case of children, examination should be explained to the accompanying adult/parent/guardian (the child should not feel that her/his wishes are getting ignored)
- palpation of the breast by either medical or nursing staff should not be included as part of routine health screening for women.

General practitioners are at an increased risk if they carry out this examination at a home visit where no other person is present.

Breast Examination

Breast examination is performed in gynaecology or family planning, either as a screening procedure or as a diagnostic one in a woman with relevant symptoms. In pregnancy there is no evidence to support routine breast examination in asymptomatic pregnant women. Breast examination may be required in puerperium when engorgement, mastitis and breast abscesses become more common.

Verbal consent must be obtained prior to examination. Personal comments should be avoided during the examination.

Part 5: Consent to the Treatment Process for Competent or Incompetent Adults

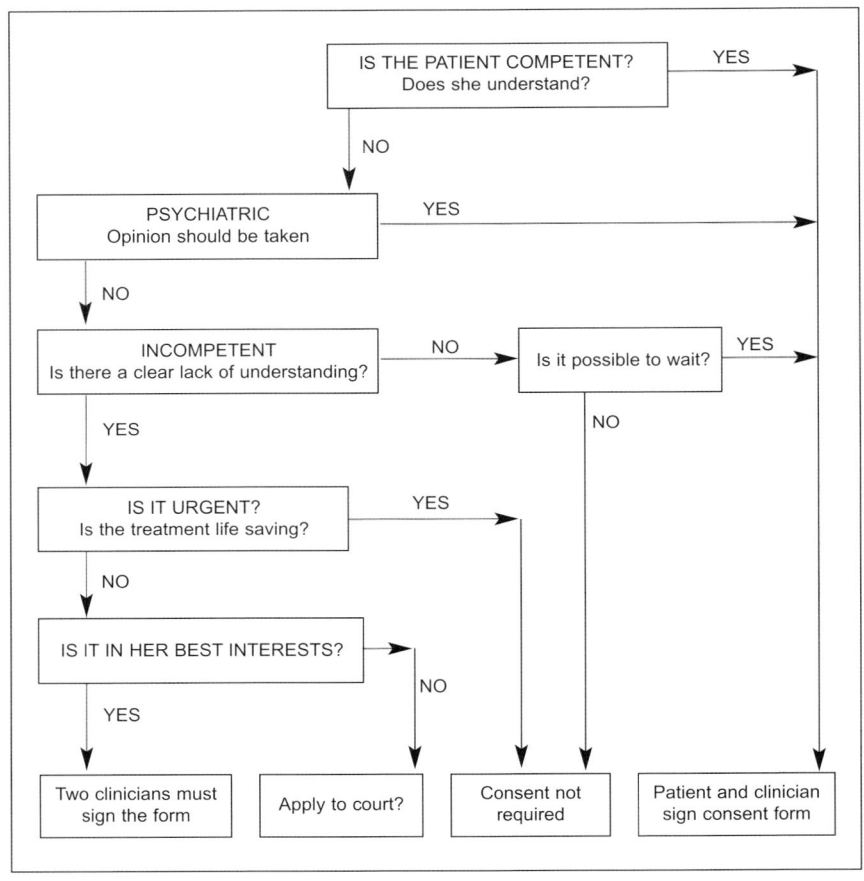

Figure 3: Flow chart showing stepwise procedure for obtaining consent

Part 6: Education and Research

Consent in Research and Medical Education

Anyone in the medical field involved in research of any kind should be aware of the general principles that govern consent in research.[30] (Consent has to be informed and written. Consent should not be oral or implied in this particular situation.)

Most of the guidance applied in medical research is a reaction to incidents during World War II. The salient features are:[31]

- The patient must have full information and give voluntary consent.
- The experiment should be designed to yield fruitful results for the good of the society.
- Research should be based on thorough knowledge of scientific literature, other relevant sources of information, and adequate laboratory and appropriate animal experimentation.
- The natural history of the disease should be such as to increase the likelihood of the benefits of research on humans.
- Avoid all unnecessary physical and mental suffering.
- There should not be a reason to believe that the experiment may harm or kill the subject.
- Risk should not exceed the benefit.
- Preparations should be proper and all efforts should be made to protect the subjects.
- Only scientifically qualified persons should take consent.
- At any time the human subject may wish to withdraw or quit and that should be made clear to the patient.
- The scientist should terminate the experiment as soon as he realises that the experiment may harm the patient.
- It is the duty of the doctor (conducting the research) to protect the life, health, dignity, integrity, privacy, and confidentiality of personal information of the individual participating in the research.
- The protocol regarding design and performance of research should be clearly defined with ethical approval and declaration. It should include information regarding funding, sponsors, institutional affiliations, and other potential conflicts of interest, incentives for subjects and provisions for treating and/or compensating subjects who are harmed as a consequence of participation in the research study. The research protocol must be submitted for consideration, comment, guidance and approval to a research ethics committee before the study begins. No change to the protocol may be made without consideration and approval by the committee.

- Research must only be conducted by individuals with the appropriate scientific training and qualifications.
- Consent must be obtained for the collection, analysis, storage and/or reuse of human material or data. Where consent is difficult, validity of the research is threatened and approval of an ethics committee is required.
- Consent should not be taken under duress because of a close relationship. In such situations, informed consent should be obtained by an appropriately qualified individual who is completely independent.
- In cases of an incompetent individual who is physically or mentally incapable of giving consent (unconscious patients), informed consent from the legally authorized representative is required. If no such representative is available and the research cannot be delayed, it may proceed without informed consent. However, reasons for involving the subject should be stated and the study must be approved by a research ethics committee.
- Patient should be fully informed about which aspects of the care are related to the research, and can refuse to participate at any time.
- Information when available should be made public.

Voluntary consent of the human subject is absolutely essential. The requirements are for a voluntary, informed, prospective consent from a person who has legal capacity, with the quality of that consent being ascertained by the experimenters themselves.

In the decades following the Second World War, two more unethical research studies have received wide publicity, the Tuskegee experiment[32] and the NZ Cervical Cancer Research.[33] In both these trials subjects from minority groups were used in an unethical manner. The outcries following these trials led to a greater awareness amongst the researchers, judiciary and human rights activists involved in the process of enforcing rights for the research subjects.

In the present day and age it would be shameful if such instances were ever repeated. It is also probably very unwise for a doctor to even stray from the tight rope of fully informed consent in medical research, even for reasons that may be considered overriding.

The UK currently follows the guidance from the Medical Research Council (MRC). These guidelines clearly emphasise that fully informed consent is a must. Furthermore, the subject has to be given sufficient time to take a decision.[34]

The Belmont Report, US (1979)

On 12 July 1974, the US National Commission for the Protection of Human Subjects of Biomedical and Behavioural Research was created by the US National Research Act. The Commission was to:
- identify the basic ethical principles that should underlie the conduct
- develop guidelines so that the research is conducted in accordance with the basic ethical principles.

The principles are:

1. Respect for Persons
   - autonomy of individuals
   - persons with diminished autonomy are entitled to protection
2. Beneficence
   - respect a person's decisions and protect them from harm
   - maximize possible benefits and minimize possible harms
3. Justice
   - benefits and risks of research must be distributed fairly.

These criteria are applied to the selection of subjects, risks and benefits assessment and informed consent.

The view of the hospital specialists in medical ethics must be taken in formulating the methodology of research locally. A well-planned and fully informed consent is a must, whatever the views of the researchers. Usually a detailed consent form is a prerequisite of starting research on a patient. Also, most institutions would recommend a brochure or other written material, which the patient can peruse at their own leisure.[35]

Research in Children

Children require special protection and may not have the capacity to give consent, which is required from the parent or legal guardian. The research should be at least as beneficial (or is supposed to be by means of prior research) when compared to the other intervention under consideration. It may also be possible to obtain consent for a treatment which, if not beneficial, is at least not detrimental to the best interests of the child. The intervention should involve minimal burden to the child.

The principles of all MRC-funded research involving children are:[36]

- Children should only be included where the relevant knowledge cannot be obtained by research in adults.
- Consent from parents/guardian is required, but if possible informed consent should be taken from competent children.
- A child upset by the procedure or who refuses to participate or continue should always be respected.
- No pressure by parents should be exerted, leading a child to volunteer in the expectation of direct benefit (therapeutic or financial).
- Obtaining consent is a continuing process rather than a one-off occurrence. Children and their families are likely to appreciate some recognition of their role in this partnership, such as a certificate of participation.
- Researchers must take account of the cumulative medical, emotional, social and psychological consequences to the child.

Research in Patients Lacking Competence

It may be ethical to carry out research involving minimal intervention on an incapable adult, if certain criteria are met. Research is the only way for mankind to enhance its knowledge, but to do so in a manner which is not consistent with human rights is unacceptable.

The key principles are:[37]

- Research must have the approval of the research ethics committee, relate to the condition and it must not be against the best interests of the given individual.
- The interests of the individual must always outweigh those of science and society.
- It is not possible to conduct equally effective research with adults who have the capacity to consent.
- The potential benefits outweigh the risks.
- If possible, consent and views should be taken from the individual close to the participant.
- A patient should be included only when there are no indications that he or she has an objection.

Consent in Medical Education

Teaching and training is a very important aspect in medicine to maintain high quality standards of care, therefore medical students and postgraduate trainees must be taught to perform pelvic examinations. The consultant must explain to the patient what is going to happen. Informed consent should be obtained and assurance given that the examination will be done in a gentle and skilled manner by the trainee. Prior written consent of the patient must be obtained in case an examination is performed by a trainee under anaesthesia.

It is accepted that explicit consent of patients is required for the presence of medical students in such places:
- 'sitting in' during gynaecological and obstetric consultations
- in operating theatres as observers and assistants
- performing clinical pelvic examinations in both conscious and anaesthetised patients.

Students

Patients should be asked if they object to being observed or treated by students. It should be clearly stated that all patients have the right to refuse this without detriment to the care they receive. It is good practice to include this in patient information leaflets, appointment cards, etc. and on posters in the waiting and ward areas.

Patients must also know the identity and the status of the student(s) who carry out an assessment or treatment. If the student is required to see a patient on an unsupervised one-to-one basis, he/she must introduce themselves and first get the permission of the patient to the consultation.

All medical students and any school or college students on work placement must register with the student's own Postgraduate Centre.

The practice of most consultants to introduce a student who is already seated in the consulting room brings about a significant element of finality to the situation. A patient may assume that she has no say in this matter. The patient must feel that she has been given a genuine choice and that she has then consented to a student's presence. Any examination that the patient undergoes has to be supervised and she must have given consent to her examination by a student. She should have understood that it is a student who is going to examine her and that she has the right to refuse. If she gives consent, the consultant must ensure that she or he examines the patient before or after the student, and that decisions have not been based solely on the student's examination.

The patient must never feel that they have been forced or their privacy invaded. Generally the patients know that they are very important in teaching and that they play an important role. When the students need to see patient records it may be a sound practice to ask the patient first. Many patients feel that the records are extra confidential.[38]

It has been shown that taking consent improves patient satisfaction and participation. The aim should be to inform the patient, make the interaction more positive, and facilitate informed consent. Special needs must be considered, for example, how it is best to communicate with those who speak different languages, have a limited ability to communicate, or have learning disabilities. A person's capacity to understand may be more limited when they are unwell, and this should be allowed for.

Recordings and Photography

There are guidelines from the Department of Health concerning consent, but they do not specifically deal with medical education. The few key points below help to serve as a guide in medical education. Ensure that:

- There is enough information in a form that can be understood about what is being asked for their consent.
- There is the opportunity to communicate.
- Feedback is valued.
- The tutor has an open, approachable attitude.

Consultations and operations may be recorded and documented for teaching or other educational purposes. Before this is carried out the patient must give their informed consent. The consent form should be signed and duly filled in or clearly documented in the notes.[38, 39] However, in some situations photography might be legitimately required at a time when the patient is unable to give consent (under anaesthesia). In these circumstances the next of kin can be approached or photographs should be withheld until retrospective informed consent has been obtained. If a patient does not agree then the photographs must be destroyed. The recording should not be used against the interest of the patient.

Verbal discussion is very important in making them aware of all the pros and cons. If consent has been given for the recording or photograph to be used in a particular way and for a particular purpose, it cannot be used for any other purpose without further consent.

To summarise:[39]

1. It is recommended that medical photography/illustration departments have a policy and protocol covering informed consent.
2. Informed consent must always be obtained for any form of audiovisual recording of the patient.
3. Informed consent should be obtained by the patient's clinician.
4. The photographer must always check that the patient understands what they have consented to.
5. If the patient changes their mind after receiving information from the photographer, then their wishes should be respected and the clinician informed.
6. It is considered good practice to provide patients with written information that clearly lays out procedures and possible uses of the photographs.
7. All audiovisual material should be clearly marked with the level of consent.
8. Informed consent should be sought for each specific use and is not generic.

Part 7: Consent Related to Blood Transfusion

Consent for Patients who Refuse Blood Transfusion

The groups of patients who refuse blood transfusion include mainly Jehovah's Witnesses and individuals who fear blood-borne infection and other risks of transfusion.[42, 43]

Jehovah's Witnesses are a religious denomination founded in the USA in 1872. Their belief is that to be transfused with blood is equivalent to eating it and is prohibited by scripture. Since 2000, the congregation no longer initiates revoking membership. However, a member who wilfully and without regret accepts blood transfusion revokes his membership by his/her own actions.

Although primary components of blood (RBC, WBC, platelets and plasma) must be refused, a Jehovah's Witness could conscientiously decide upon the primary components herself. There are no absolute rules and some Jehovah's Witnesses may accept plasma protein fraction or components such as albumin. Every individual patient should be asked about their personal interpretation of treatment options in a one-to-one consultation. Significant variation exists among Jehovah's Witnesses over their willingness to accept specific blood products and treatment alternatives.

Every attempt should be made to value a woman's wishes whilst giving information to enable her to participate in her care. A detailed account of the woman's wishes should be documented following discussion of the options.[44, 45]

- All decisions regarding care should be documented.
- Women who decline blood products should be seen as early as possible in the pregnancy to ascertain their views on blood transfusion.
- A woman should be given up-to-date information of the options available to her.
- A multidisciplinary approach is the mainstay of her care.
- In addition, a standardized procedure of informed consent outlining the different treatment alternatives will permit the clinician to meet the specific needs of a pregnant Jehovah's Witness, and to ensure that her wishes are respected and the best possible outcome achieved.
- Blood substitute can be used for those who decline blood products, and various other measures can be instigated to minimise anaemia

and blood loss (such as oral iron, iron dextran, recombinant erythropoetin, preliminary ligation of major vessels, intra-operative salvage and re-infusion, volume expanders etc.)

- Alternatives to allogeneic blood and blood products are crystalloids, colloids, erythropoetin, cell-saver device, homeostatic drugs such as antifibrinolytics or aprotinin.
- Labour should be conducted in an acute unit. A senior obstetrician should be informed when a woman is admitted in labour. Active management of labour should be encouraged.
- If operative delivery is required then a senior obstetrician and an anaesthetist should be involved at an earlier stage.
- In cases of haemorrhage, a woman and her family must be informed of events in a non-judgemental way. Because uterine atony is the most common cause of postpartum haemorrhage, different uterotonic agents (oxytocin, methylergonovine, carboprost tromethamine, and misoprostol) should be available. Other intra-operative techniques such as uterine artery ligation, hypogastric artery ligation, or B-lynch stitch should be used for atony not responding to medical management.[45]
- Hysterectomy should be considered earlier in cases of severe haemorrhage.
- Cell-salvage (saver) systems may play a role in the management of pregnant Jehovah's Witnesses and can be regarded as a form of intra-operative autologous blood donation. Some Jehovah's Witnesses will agree to cell-saver technology; others may not find it acceptable.
- Controlled hypotensive anesthesia is another technique that aims at reducing the mean arterial pressure to 50 mmHg, which minimizes the blood loss in cases of massive intra-operative haemorrhage.
- Hyperbaric oxygen therapy may have a role in management.
- In the acute management of a major obstetric haemorrhage, recombinant factor VIIa (rFVIIa) may be used. It is a synthetic product that is not derived from blood and is accepted by many Jehovah's Witnesses.[47]

A doctor may lawfully give treatment that is thought to be necessary and in the best interests of the woman only if the woman is deemed to be incompetent. It should be clear that while competent she would not have refused consent to a particular treatment. In principle, an appropriate refusal to consent to blood products form should be completed.

Specific Checklist for the Management of Pregnant Women who Decline Transfusions

Prenatal Care
- Comprehensive discussion with a checklist specifying acceptable interventions
- Aggressively prevent anaemia (goal: HCT: 36–40%)
- Iron – PO or IV (sucrose) with folate and B12 as needed
- rh-Erythropoietin 600 units/kg SQ 1–3x per weekly as needed (most preparations have 2.5 ml of albumin so may be refused by some Jehovah's Witnesses)
- Line up consultants (consider maternal fetal medicine consultant, hematology, anesthesiology).

Labour and Delivery
- Anaesthesia consultation early
- Reassessment of haemorrhage risk and discussion of options (e.g. surgery, interventional radiology)
- Review specific techniques (e.g. options checklist and fibrin/thrombin glues, rFactor VIIa – but remember that rFVIIa needs factors to work)
- Review references – have a Plan!
- Be decisive.

Postpartum
- Maintain volume with crystalloids and blood substitutes
- Aggressively treat anemia
- Iron – IV (sucrose)
- Rh-Erythropoietin 600 units/kg SQ weekly (3x week)[48]

Unconscious Haemorrhaging Adult
- If time permits, any previous documented evidence of the patient stating refusal of blood transfusion should be examined.
- A copy should be put in the notes and its contents should be respected.
- A senior doctor (consultant) should discuss with the patient's relative the implications of withholding blood.
- A doctor should act in the best interests of the patient and will be expected to perform to the best of their ability, which may involve giving blood if the above steps are impossible. A clear and signed entry of the steps taken should be written in the patient's case notes.

Transfusion for Children of Jehovah's Witness

- Medical and nursing staff are not legally required to obtain consent before providing life-saving treatment to a child against their parent's wishes.
- Two senior doctors should make an unambiguous, clear and signed entry in the clinical record that blood transfusion is essential or likely to become so to save life or prevent serious, permanent harm.
- Access to legal advice should be attempted through the hospital trust solicitor. Parents should be informed so they may be properly represented at consequent hearings. People with parental responsibility for babies and young children are legally empowered to refuse treatment on their behalf until they can consent for themselves.
- Where there is conflict between parental refusal and the medical/nursing opinion regarding what is in the best interests of the child, the matter should be referred to the court as above.
- Children of 16–18 years have a statutory right to consent to treatment on their own behalf. Where a child of any age has sufficient understanding and intelligence to make their own decision about treatment, their consent is valid and cannot be overruled by parental objection.
- If a child deemed to be Gillick competent refuses a blood transfusion, the matter can be referred to the courts as above.[50]

Part 8: Elements of a Surgical Procedure and Consent to Anaesthesia

The Patient
The patient should be suitable for the surgery (i.e. the procedure should be appropriately selected for the patient with clear indication of the benefits and with minimal harm). The patient should be fit for the operation. Although there is a clear benefit from the particular operation, if the patient's condition does not allow the procedure to be performed safely, alternative measures should be sought.

Full surgical and anaesthetic risk assessment should be carried out before the operation with appropriate investigations performed and consultation of the other specialists such as a cardiologist if needed.

The Surgery
The operation should be suitable for the patient and appropriately selected with minimal risk as compared to other available options. In life-saving procedures the benefits outweigh any given risk.

The Surgeon (same rules apply to anaesthetists)
He/she should:
- be adequately trained for the given procedure
- be adequately supervised if in training
- recognise the limits of professional competence (GMC requirement)
- be on a continuous personal development plan
- call for help in appropriate time, help could be sought from a colleague from the same speciality or from other disciplines such as urology.

Some procedures require subspecialty training such as foetal medicine procedures, oncology, endoscopic surgery, etc.

The Assistant
Some procedures require an experienced assistant. This helps to reduce operation time and minimises complications. The importance of a good assistant should not be underestimated. An adequately trained paramedical person (e.g. theatre nurse or a midwife) could be as equally efficient as a doctor.

The Team
Theatre nursing and auxiliary staff should be adequately trained and familiar with instruments, equipment and suture material. This is particularly important in specialised procedures such as laparoscopic and hysteroscopic surgery or complicated procedures.

The Equipment
All theatre instruments and equipment should be regularly tested and maintained. Serial batch numbers should be recorded appropriately. An important example is the Filshie Clip and clip applicator.

The Theatre
Environment and set-up should be adequate e.g. infection control ventilation and lighting. All of these combined together make up a surgical procedure. It is important to ensure that all the components are in their best possible condition before embarking on the procedure itself. An extra few minutes before surgery may prevent hours, days or months of heartbreak.

Consent to Anaesthesia
It is imperative that consent should include consent for anaesthesia. The requirements for consent to an anaesthetic procedure are no less rigorous than for any other procedure that involves a physically invasive treatment to the patient. The anaesthetist has a clear duty to give the patient an explanation of what he/she intends to do, the potential risks and benefits, and to obtain consent.

Information about types of anaesthesia and pain relief should be given to the patient before the day of the operation.

Recommendations outlined in the Association of Anaesthetists of Great Britain and Ireland Working Party Report, July 1999 should be followed, and all anaesthetists should familiarise themselves with this document.[51]

On the advice of the Working Party, the treating anaesthetist will document the discussion about anaesthetic technique and associated risks with the patient on the anaesthetic record.

The consent form includes a paragraph indicating that the patient will have an opportunity to discuss the type of anaesthetic and anaesthetic procedure involved with an anaesthetist prior to the operation.

In procedures done under local anaesthesia/sedation the concerned clinician will be personally responsible for ensuring that the patient has given proper consent.

Part 9: Consent to Screening

Screening is a test applied to a healthy or asymptomatic population to detect genetic predisposition or early signs of disease. A screening test is not a definitive test, therefore there are uncertainties involved (the risk of false positive or false negative results). The result of screening may have potentially serious medical, social or financial consequences, which is not only limited to individuals but can also affect their families.

It is important that anyone considered for screening should be adequately informed so that informed consent can be obtained. Attention should be paid particularly to ensure that the information given to the person is relevant and adequate to her requirement.

Careful and clear explanation should include:
- the purpose of the screening
- the likelihood of positive/negative findings and possibility of false positive/negative results
- the uncertainties and risks attached to the screening process
- any significant medical, social or financial implications of screening for the particular condition or predisposition
- follow-up plans, including availability of counselling and support services.

Counselling for Antenatal Screening

Antenatal screening is widely used in modern obstetrics and gynaecology. In recent decades antenatal screening has become one of the most routine procedures in pregnancy and the subject of hot debate in bioethics circles.[52, 53, 54]

Many would say that antenatal screening is performed unthoughtfully, pregnancy is treated almost as a disease since the emergence of antenatal screening, and it is more to do with the interests of others rather than those of the child-to-be.

Recent studies[52, 53, 54] have indicated that the major paediatric health problems are handicaps due to genetic disorder or congenital malformation. When it was noticed that more than a quarter of all deaths in the first year of life was due to fetal abnormality, scientists were alarmed and parents sought a 'remedy' for the 'problem'.

Although antenatal diagnostic techniques were initially described in the nineteenth century, it was not until the middle of the twentieth century that the techniques were applied to screening and management of various genetic disorders and congenital malformations. Antenatal screening and diagnostic techniques are almost the norm; probably around 90% of women in the UK have undergone one of these at some time during pregnancy.

Counselling, before and after antenatal screening, is crucial.

- Ideal counselling involves informing the parents that there is no 'right' decision to be made, and whatever their decision is, they will be supported.
- They must also be clear about whether it is a screening test or a diagnostic test, and how accurate it is in their particular situation.
- They need to be aware of the risks involved in the pregnancy and the possible consequences of dealing with the information that the test provides.
- Medical professionals should discuss the feasibility, accuracy and clear-cut details of any such tests, including the dangers and the method of termination if they choose to terminate the pregnancy following an abnormal result.
- It is known that it is very difficult for a woman to decline antenatal screening when offered.
- Doctors should not impose their own moral attitudes upon their patients. If there is disagreement with the moral stance of their patients, they should explain their situation and advise the patients to consult a clinical geneticist.

To provide this kind of ideal counselling there must be enough well-trained healthcare professionals who offer suitable training opportunities and satisfy the expectations of users of screening services.

'Genetic counselling' includes (pre-conception and post-conception), advising adults of the probability of their conceiving a child with a genetic disorder.

The most important development is public awareness and education. It is argued that the conflict of interests between providers and users of antenatal screening services is clearly reflected in the counselling process. At all stages of screening, counselling is systematically biased towards encouraging women to take up the tests and have an abortion if an abnormality is detected, rather than providing women with the information and support they require to make an informed choice and to avoid unnecessary distress.

Women undergoing routine antenatal screening are generally under-informed about the tests that they are being offered.[55]

Apart from the failure to provide enough information, the bias toward termination of pregnancy in the event of abnormality detection is another controversy in screening procedure. The medical profession generally concedes that the primary aim of antenatal diagnosis is the detection and subsequent abortion, of abnormal fetuses. Because of the procedural risks to the fetus and the lack of effective methods of fetal therapy for most malformations, antenatal diagnosis is a rational activity only if abortion is seen as an acceptable alternative. However, some people may consider this kind of approach to prenatal diagnosis not only unfair, but also rather unethical.

Despite all improvements, screening is not 100% accurate. It is reported that: "Routine screening tests do not detect all cases. MS-AFP detects about 80% of cases of spina bifida. Although smaller, there is a false negative rate from both CVS and amniocentesis. All screening tests have an inherent risk of being false positive."[56]

The routine use of ultrasound may result in the detection of symptomless minor anomalies. The incidence and natural history of these are unknown. Although these are not indications for a termination, their detection means that women can face the rest of their pregnancy with the knowledge that their child has an abnormality whose implications are unknown. This may have two different consequences: the diagnosis of a possible abnormality may affect the acceptance of the baby by the parents and create negative attitudes in them towards it; or it may alert parents to prepare emotionally and psychologically for their (possibly) handicapped baby.

For all couples with an abnormal result, there may be moral or religious objections or social pressures surrounding termination. There may be disagreements between the couple as to the correct course of action. It is not always possible to give the couple a clear idea of the particular disability of that particular fetus. There is also the extremely important emotional consequence of the decision, a feeling of responsibility for the loss of a wanted child, which many couples describe as guilt. Clearly in these situations, the decision-making is more difficult, and for those couples who choose to terminate a pregnancy at less than 100% risk of the fetus being affected, there will be lingering doubts about whether the baby might, after all, have been normal.

It is possible that some screening programmes currently do more harm than good.[59]

Live born children with an uncomplicated abdominal wall defect, for example, have an excellent chance of survival and a negligible risk of long-term disability, but antenatal diagnosis can bring with it ill-justified pressure for the pregnancy to be terminated.

From all these discussions it becomes apparent that non-directive counselling is a myth. Today, counselling is directive, and its direction is towards having antenatal screening and going to termination if something is wrong with the 'baby in the womb'.

Consent to Blood-Borne Virus Testing (HIV Antibody, Hepatitis C Antibody, Hepatitis B Surface Antigen)

Patients should be given appropriate information about the implications of such testing, including advantages and disadvantages. There should be appropriate and enough time given to consider and discuss the test and its implications in detail.

Information leaflets should be given after providing all the information so that the patient can make an informed choice, having first understood the implications of testing for herself and her unborn child. For example, a leaflet about screening for hepatitis B should provide information about the infection and health implications for the baby, the mother and close contacts. A number of local leaflets are already available offering information on antenatal screening in conjunction with the DoH. Such leaflets will also emphasise the importance of a complete course of immunisation to protect the baby. Hepatitis B virus affects the liver and in many people has no symptoms, therefore a blood test is offered universally to identify those cases. Most adults infected with the virus recover fully but 10% become carriers and affect others. In 20% of these, carriers develop serious disease in later life.

Infection is usually acquired by sexual intercourse and direct contact with the blood of an infected person (sharing a toothbrush, razors, body piercing and tattooing instruments, or a drug user sharing needles/syringes), is passed from the mother to her baby, or most importantly, needlestick injury in health professionals.

If a healthcare worker has suffered a needlestick injury or has been exposed to blood or body fluids from a patient, written consent should be obtained from the patient before testing for blood-borne viruses. If such a patient is unable to consent or refuses to do so, then testing should only be performed in exceptional circumstances.

Advice should be sought from the hospital trust's occupational health department. If blood is taken for testing from an unconscious patient consent should be sought once the patient has regained full consciousness. If the patient remains unconscious for more than 48 hours, the severity of risk should carefully be assessed and, again, further advice should be sought from the occupational health department. If the patient is deemed incompetent to give consent, the procedure as stated in the 'Incompetent Adults' section of the guidance[59] should be followed, again with advice from the occupational health department. In the case of needlestick injury from a deceased patient, advice should be sought from the occupational health department.

Part 10: Steps Taken to Avoid Complaints

Avoid Communication Breakdown

Breakdown of communication between the patient and the healthcare professional is a critical factor leading to malefactor litigation. Communications and attitude are the primary reason for patients pursuing a malpractice in the majority of cases. It is a perception of some patients and their relatives that doctors are arrogant, cannot communicate, and make little attempt to explain to patients about their illness or show concern about their welfare as people.

Avoid Jargon

Use of medical jargon that patients do not understand, technical language (e.g. 'oedema') and medical shorthand (e.g. 'history') should be avoided. Write and think clearly.

Show Empathy

The media always report dissatisfaction with the doctor-patient relationship. They comment on doctors' poor understanding of the patient as a person with individual concerns and wishes. It is perceived that physicians lack warmth and friendliness, which leads to patient dissatisfaction and complaints. Being nice to the patient is a very simple way to avoid litigation.

Taking Training

Training in relationship building skills, breaking bad news and the ability to communicate empathetically have become part of the curriculum of the health professional. Training should be given to the doctors on how to establish eye contact so that emotional distress can be detected in patients. Training in handling emotion is important in the detection of psychological problems.

Understand the Patient's Perspective

It is very important knowing how to take a history of a patient's illness. Patient-centeredness in the interview leads to greater satisfaction. Discovering and acknowledging the patient's satisfaction improves it. Opportunity should be given to the patient to discuss their health concerns rather than to simply answer the questions.

Be Comfortable with Assertiveness

This means not losing your temper but also standing up for your rights. It is a delicate balance but nevertheless one we all must strike.

Risk Management

Despite the attention given to risk management and avoidance of adverse incidents in other fields of endeavour, the NHS has clearly lagged behind. Reporting of adverse events has been haphazard and there is no reliable, systematic way of identifying lapses, analysing them and learning from them.

While preventing the repetition of serious accidents is clearly important, lowering the incidence of less serious but much more frequent events is at least equally important. Errors can never be entirely eliminated. It is suggested that 70% of adverse events are preventable, so that the dividends to be gained in terms of relief of human suffering and costs to the NHS are potentially enormous.[58, 59]

Cultural Change

Cultural change in the NHS is necessary to minimise litigation. This requires a considerable cultural change across the whole organisation. The changes required are critically dependent on full, open reporting of adverse events and 'near misses'. While reaction to such incidents continues to include 'naming and shaming' coupled with punitive disciplinary action, little will be achieved in the prevention of similar events in the future.

Heavy emphasis is laid on organisational systems. Implementation of local clinical governance, working within national guidance provided through national service frameworks, NICE guidelines, performance assessment, professional standards and guidelines prepared by colleges and specialist societies should all provide the necessary framework. The incident reporting should be a continuous process of monitoring, rather than short-term responses to specific events.

The Chief Medical Officer's report clearly outlines the barriers to achieving success and emphasises the need for organisations to develop a culture in which strong features include encouragement to report, flexibility, a sense of justice, and learning. Winning hearts and minds will not be easy, especially in an NHS where inadequate numbers of nurses, doctors and beds make everyone work at and beyond the limits of their capacity.

Clinicians should be persuaded to report adverse events and told that they will be helped and supported, whether they are at fault or not. This will be no easy task in our litigation prone age. Whistle blowing, although important where malpractice is a possibility, is not likely to be helpful in the context of the majority of incidents.

Use Leaflets

Leaflets, explanations with diagrams and informed consent are paramount in preventing litigation. All hospitals use information leaflets produced locally, by the DoH and from other organisations. Royal College guidelines and protocols are important to practice evidence-based medicine and keep up-to-date in the management care of patient.

References

1. Green V. *Liability in Obstetrics and Gynaecology.* Chapter 43. http://www.ablminc.org/Model_Curriculum_LMME_2010/BOOK_Le gal%20Medicine-7th_2007/Ch43Liability%20in%20Obstetrics%-20And%20Gynecology.pdf (accessed 16/9/11).
2. The NHS Litigation Authority. *Factsheet 3: information on claims.* http://www.nhsla.com/NR/.../NHSLAFactsheetclaimsinformation20 0708.doc (accessed 16/9/11). 2011.
3. Mayberry M & Mayberry J. *Consent in Clinical Practice.* Abingdon: Radcliffe Medical Press.1993.
4. GMC. *Guidance for Doctors. Confidentiality: protecting and providing information.*http://www.gmcuk.org/static/documents/ content/Confidentiality_0910.pdf. (accessed 16/9/11). 2009.
5. DOH. *Reference Guide to Consent for Examination or Treatment.* (2nd edn).http://www.dh.gov.uk/prod_consum_dh/groups/dh_ digitalassets/documents/digitalasset/dh_103653.pdf (accessed 16/9/11). 2009.
6. GMC. *Seeking Patients'Consent:theethicalconsiderations.* http://www.gmcuk.org/Seeking_patients_consent_The_ethical _considerations.pdf_25417085.pdf (accessed 16/9/11). 1998.
7. GMC. *Guidance for Doctors. Confidentiality: protecting and providing information.* http://www.gmcuk.org/static/documents/ content/Confidentiality_0910.pdf. (accessed 16/9/11). 2009.
8. Edwards KA. *Ethics in Medicine.* http://depts.washington.edu/bioethx/topics/consent.html (accessed 16/9/11). 1998.
9. *Bolam v. Friern Hospital Management Committee* [1957] 2 All ER 118.
10. Jones JW. The healthcare professional and the Bolam test. *British Dental Journal.* 2000, 188(5): 237–40.
11. *Lord Woolf: Kralj v. McGrath* [1986] 1 All ER 54.

12. GMC. *Guidance for Doctors. Confidentiality: protecting and providing information.* http://www.gmc-uk.org/static/documents /content/Confidentiality_0910.pdf (accessed 16/9/11). 2009.

13. *Freedom of Information Act 2000.* Access to information held by public authorities. London: The Stationary Office Ltd. 2000. (Scotland has different Act.)

14. *Data Protection Act 1998.*

15. *Mental Health Act 2007.*

16 Nuffield Council on Bioethics. *Critical Care Decisions on Fetal and Neonatal Medicine: ethical issues.* http://www.nuffieldbioethics.org/sites/default/files/CCD%20web% 20version%2022%20June%2007%20(updated).pdf   (accessed 16/9/11). 2006.

17. *DOH. Reference Guide to Consent for Examination or Treatment. (2nd edn).* http://www.dh.gov.uk/prod_consum_dh/groups/dh_digitalassets/do cuments/digitalasset/dh_103653.pdf (accessed 16/9/11). 2009.

18. GMC. *0–18 years: guidance for all doctors.* http://www.gmc-uk.org/guidance/ethical_guidance/children_guidance_contents.as p (accessed 16/9/11). 2007.

19. *Gillick v. Wisbech and West Norfolk AHA* [1985] 3 All ER 402.

20. DOH. *The Effective Commissioning of Sexual Health and HIV Services.*http://www.dh.gov.uk/prod_consum_dh/groups/dh_digital assets/@dh/@en/documents/digitalasset/dh_4084695.pdf (accessed 16/9/11). 2003.

21. BMA et al. *Confidentiality and People under 16.* London: BMA, GMSC, HEA, Brook Advisory Centres, FPA and RCGP. 1994.

22. *Mental Capacity Act 2005.* Lasting powers of Attorney, Enduring powers of Attorney and public Guardian Regulations 2007, http://www.legislation.gov.uk/uksi/2007/1253/made?view=plain (accessed 16/9/11).

23. DOH. *12 Key Points on Consent: the law in England.* http://www.dh.gov.uk/prod_consum_dh/groups/dh_digitalassets/@ dh/@en/documents/digitalasset/dh_075159.pdf   (accessed 16/9/11). 2001.

24. *Human Tissue Act.*

25. Medical Research Council. *Human Tissue and Biological Samples for use in Research – Operational and Ethical Guidelines.* http://www.mrc.ac.uk/Utilities/Documentrecord/index.htm?d=MRC 002420 (accessed 16/9/11). 2001.

26. RCOG. *Gynaecological Examinations: guidelines for specialist practice.* http://www.rcog.org.uk/files/rcog-corp/uploaded-files/WPRGynaeExams2002.pdf (accessed16/9/11). 2002.

27. Speelman A, Savage J & Verburgh M. Use of chaperones by general practitioners. *BMJ.* 1993, 307(6910): 986–7.

28. Bignell CJ. Chaperone for genital examination. *BMJ.* 1999, 319(7203): 137–8.

29. GMC. *Maintaining Boundaries: guidance for doctors.* http://www.gmc-uk.org/guidance/ethical_guidance/maintaining_boundaries.asp (accessed 16/9/11). 2006.

30. Clinical trials are covered by the *Medicines for Human Use (Clinical Trials) Regulations 2004.*

31. Word Medical Association. *WMA Declaration of Helsinki – Ethical Principles for Medical Research Involving Human Subjects.* http://www.wma.net/en/30publications/10policies/b3/ (accessed 16/9/11). 2008.

32. Jones JH. *Bad blood: the Tuskegee syphilis experiment.* New York: The Free Press.1981.

33. Rosier P. The speculum bites back: feminists spark an inquiry into the treatment of carcinoma in situ at Auckland's National Women's Hospital. *Reprod Genet Eng.*1989, 2(2): 121–32.

34. Medical Research Council. *Clinical Trials Regulations 2004.*

35. GMC. *Good Practice in Research and Consent to Research.* http://www.gmc-uk.org/guidance/ethical_guidance/5991.asp (accessed 16/9/11). 2010.

36. Medical Research Council. *Medical Research Involving Children.* http://www.mrc.ac.uk/Utilities/Documentrecord/index.htm?d=MRC002430 (accessed 16/9/11). 2004.

37. Medical Research Council. *MRC Ethics Guide: medical research involving adults who cannot consent.* http://www.mrc.ac.uk/Utilities/Documentrecord/index.htm?d=MRC002409 (accessed 16/9/11). 2007.

38. Carman D & Britten N. Confidentiality of medical records: the patient's perspective. *British Journal of General Practice.*1995, 45(398): 485–8.

39. GMC. *Making and Using Visual and Audio Recordings of Patients.* http://www.gmc-uk.org/guidance/ethical_guidance/making_audiovisual.asp (accessed 16/9/11). 2011.

40. Hove A & Anderson J. Involving patients in medical education. *BMJ.* 2003, 327(7410): 326–8.

41. Institute of Medical Illustrators. *IMI National Guidelines. Consent to Clinical Photography.* http://www.imi.org.uk/file/download/2143/IMINatGuidelines ConsentMarch_2007.pdf (accessed 16/9/11). 2006.

42. Bennett DR & Shulman IA. Practical issues when confronting a patient who refuses blood transfusion therapy. *Am J Clin Pathol.* 1997, 107 (4 Suppl 1): S23–7.

43. Finfer S et al. Managing patients who refuse blood transfusions: an ethical dilemma. *BMJ.* 1994, 308(6941): 1423–6.

44. RCOG. Care plan for women in labour refusing blood transfusions. *RCOG News.* 7(4) 2000.

45. Gyamfi C & Berkowitz RL. Responses by pregnant Jehovah's Witnesses on health care proxies. *Obstet Gynecol.* 2004, 104(3): 541–4.

46. Mirza FG & Gyamfi C. Management of pregnancy in the Jehovah's Witness. *ModernMedicine.* http://www.modernmedicine.com/modernmedicine/Modern+Medicine+Now/Management-of-pregnancy-in-the-Jehovahs-Witness/ArticleStandard/Article/detail/697972 (accessed 16/9/11). 1 December 2010.

47. Laird R & Carabine U. Recombinant factor VIIa for major obstetric haemorrhage in a Jehovah's Witness. *Int J Obstet Anesth.* 2008, 17(2): 193–4.

48. Main E. *Checklist for Management of Pregnant Women Who Refuse Transfusions.* CMQCC OB Haemorrhage Task Force. Download via: http://www.cmqcc.org/resources/ob_haemorrhage/ob_haemorrhage_tools_jehovah_s_witness (accessed 16/9/11). 03/12/2009.

49. Main E. *Blood Product Consent* (Jehovah's Witness, Others).CMQCC OB Haemorrhage Task Force. Download via: http://www.cmqcc.org/resources/ob_haemorrhage/ob_haemorrhage_tools_jehovah_s_witness (accessed 16/9/11). 03/12/2009.

50. *Gillick v. Wisbech and West Norwich* AHA (1985) 2 All ER 402.

51. The Association of Anaesthetists of Great Britain and Ireland. *Information and Consent for Anaesthesia.* 1999.

52. Farrant W. Who's for amniocentesis? The politics of prenatal screening. In: H. Homans (ed.) *The Sexual Politics of Reproduction,* pp.96–177. London: Gower. 1985.

53. Abramsky L. Counselling prior to prenatal testing. In: L Abramsky & J Chapple (eds) *Prenatal Diagnosis: the human side.* London: Chapman and Hall.1994. (Book also has a 2003 edition.)

54. Sjogren B & Uddenberg N. Decision making during the prenatal diagnostic procedure: a question and interview study of 211 women participating in prenatal diagnosis. *Prenatal Diagnosis* 8. 1988: 263–73.

55. Marteau TM et al. Development of a self-administered questionnaire to measure women's knowledge of prenatal screening and diagnostic tests. *Journal of Psychosomatic Research.*1988, 32(4–5): 403–8.

56. Atkins AFC & Hey EN et al. The Northern regional fetal abnormality survey. In: JO Drife & D Donnai (eds.) *Antenatal Diagnosis of Fetal Abnormalities*, pp.13–30. London: Springer-Verlag.1991.

57. Wald NJ et al. Maternal serum-alpha-fetoprotein measurement in antenatal screening for anencephaly and spina bifida in early pregnancy. Report of U.K. collaborative study on alpha-fetoprotein in relation to neural-tube defects. *Lancet.* 1977, 1(8026): 1323–32.

58. DOH. *An organisation with a memory: report of an expert group on learning from adverse events in the NHS*. London: The Stationary Office. 2000.

59. Kohn LT, & Corrigan JM & Donaldson MS (eds.) *To Err is Human: building a safer health system.* Washington DC: Institute of Medicine. 2000.

CHAPTER 2: COMPLICATIONS OF OBSTETRICS PROCEDURES

Consent and Ethical Issues in Obstetrics and Gynaecology

The events and problems related to this are unique in obstetrics and gynaecology, the reasons being that all patients are female, the majority of medical practitioners are male, and the clinical concern is with the function and disorders of the female reproductive tract. This situation requires even higher standards than usual of discretion, sensitivity and professionalism in medical practice.

In many ways obstetrics is a speciality, where most of the time is spent in a leisurely and patient approach to medicine. This can change abruptly to a fast-paced, emergent surgical scenario. The change of pace can be quite upsetting at times and may lead to its own set of problems. Concern is focused on at least two patients, of whom only one (the mother) can partake in the decision-making process.

The common problems encountered are:

1. Reproduction is regarded as a fundamental human function. Society and the courts regard any irreversible interference without full information as extremely serious (e.g. the sterilisation of mentally handicapped people has raised grave issues).
2. Legality of the provision of oral contraceptives to girls under the age of 16 has been the subject of recent examination by the courts.
3. Therapeutic termination of pregnancy presents an irresolvable ethical and moral dilemma.
4. Emergencies are a feature of obstetrical practice, where the conditions for legal consent are difficult.
5. Added aspects such as serological samples retained for HIV testing, have made consenting for routine blood testing also necessary. Testing for HIV is mandatory and cannot be done without informed consent.
6. More recently, legality of the practice of medical students performing pelvic examinations on anaesthetised female patients without their knowledge has become an issue.
7. Legality over the retention and use of fetal and placental tissues for research or therapeutic use, ownership of the tissue, and the legality of surrogacy, have all been matters of concern.
8. The adequacy and nature of information given to patients when obtaining consent for sterilisation procedures has been tested in a series of failed sterilisation cases.

9. Pre-implantation genetic diagnosis, testing for genetic markers, premature diagnosis and selective abortion all cause ethical and moral dilemmas.

Consent can become quite a challenge sometimes, with neither the medical staff nor the patient having the time or the inclination to take a fully informed consent. On occasion this lack of proper communication can lead to a state of unfulfilled expectations by the mother and/or the family. As a clinician, a midwife or a nurse, one has to be very careful that all the necessary steps have been taken. At times it can be quite difficult deciding how much information has to be given, especially during a situation of profound stress. The ability to decide that, very often distinguishes a practice from one with a low to one with a high litigation rate.

Furthermore, in this practice there is the added dimension of the midwife/doctor interaction. The health practitioner acts as a source of information that can vary from very helpful to misleading, depending on the amount of importance that is given to the patient. The doctor, whether senior or junior, should remember that some midwives can be more experienced than they are themselves. Therefore, it is important to discuss consent issues with them in difficult situations when time is limited and a woman's decision-making process is clouded by the sedative/analgesics. The junior staff should especially remember this and hence, give due importance to their patient's views. Nevertheless, any decision should be taken only if it is considered right. The consequences are not shared by anyone but the person who took the decision.

With these problems in mind, special issues relating to obstetrics in general will be discussed, followed by individual diseases in particular.

Normal delivery supposes to be a normal physiological phenomenon, and it is not free of complications. Some complications are severe in nature and it can become very difficult to counsel patients on the basis that normal vaginal delivery is the safest mode of delivery. For instance, there have been problems where a patient was booked for an elective LSCS (due to a previous LSCS), progressed to normal delivery and then had perineal damage with postpartum haemorrhage.

While obtaining informed consent for routine procedures during spontaneous vaginal delivery, the following points should be considered, highlighting the associated problems.

Part 1: Complications in Spontaneous Normal Vaginal Delivery

Normal delivery is supposed to be a normal physiological phenomenon, therefore serious complications are not usually anticipated. Normal delivery can cause serious morbidity where it is least anticipated. Therefore every patient who carries a risk of developing complications should be informed fully and verbal consent should be obtained for management in an emergency situation (such as severe postpartum haemorrhage in multigravida, shoulder dystocia, failure to progress etc.). There is not one right mode of delivery for all women. All depends on the situation, the indications, the obstetricians, the midwives, the information and finally the choice of the patient.

Complications of spontaneous normal vaginal delivery are outlined below.

Immediate complications
- Emergency caesarean section   10–15%
- Bleeding more than 500 ml   5%
- Bleeding more than 1500 ml   1%
- Febrile morbidity due to endometritis   6–7%
- Perineal haematoma   1–2/1000
- Pelvic haematoma   1:300–10,000
- Perineal laceration leading to haemorrhage
- Shoulder dystocia   0.6–1.4%
- Retained placenta
- Severe maternal morbidity
- Vulva bruising perineal oedema
- Postpartum depression   18.3%
- Paragenital haematoma (infra/supralevator), vulval, ischiorectal haematoma
- Pain in symphysis pubis joint
- Multiple petechiae over face, neck and shoulder and conjunctival haemorrhage

Rare complications (less than 1/1000)
- Uterine inversion   1:20,000
- Sheehan's syndrome   1:10,000
- Spontaneous uterine rupture   1:1900
- Thromboembolism antepartum   0.6/1000
- Thromboembolism postpartum   1.3/1000

- Pulmonary embolism — 1–2/100,000
- Bladder injury — 0.003/100
- Ureteric injury — 0.001/100
- Necrotising fasciitis
- Unexplained shock, amniotic fluid embolism
- Hysterectomy — 0.01/100
- Coccygeal damage due to dislocation and displacement of fracture
- Nerve injury – peroneal, pudendal, lumbosacral
- Third and fourth degree perineal tear — 0.1%
- Maternal mortality — 6.2/100,000
- Need for further surgery — 0.03/100

Late complications
- Urinary incontinence
- Vaginal prolapse
- Anal incontinence (sphincter damage noted on endoanal scan) — 35%

Fetal complications
- Intracranial haemorrhage — 1:1900
- Clavicle fracture
- Erb's palsy (more common than caesarean section delivery)
- More risk of vertical transmission infection than elective CS

Pelvic haematoma is a rare but life-threatening condition (approximately 1:1000 requires surgical intervention). Maternal mortality due to vulvovaginal haematoma is 21%. Blood transfusion, antibiotics and aggressive surgical intervention reduce the morbidity and mortality. The incidence of thromboembolic events in pregnancy increases with operative procedure, bed rest, bleeding, sepsis, advance maternal age >40 years, multiparity, multiple gestation and being overweight. Postpartum depression can occur up to 7 months after delivery. Sheehan's syndrome is a rare complication. The incidence is probably lower than previously stated due to better management of PPH (blood transfusion).[1]

Part 2: Complications and Consent in Episiotomy

Perineal trauma has a major impact on women's health. Some of these problems may be avoided by careful repair of the trauma by an appropriately trained practitioner, whilst others are apparently unavoidable or are of unknown aetiology. What is important is that there is early recognition of these problems and women receive appropriate sensitive treatment.[2]

It is estimated that over 85% of women who have a vaginal birth will sustain some degree of perineal trauma, and of these, 60–70% will require suturing. Perineal trauma may occur spontaneously or intentionally by a surgical incision (episiotomy).

Episiotomy is a commonly performed procedure. It seems to be a part of a normal vaginal delivery and hence it is very often not given sufficient care and attention. For a patient it is an invasive procedure and can be definitely separated from the rest of the delivery.

Consent for episiotomy is not implied by the patient's presence in the hospital for maternity care. To the patient the why's, how's, when's and what's of this procedure are hazy at best, and she needs to get a complete answer to all these questions. Often the patient is given a vague explanation of a possible procedure that she may have to undergo (a vague blanket consent) at some time during her labour, or she has to concentrate on consent right in the middle of the most intensely painful period in her life. Both these situations are avoidable if a small amount of diligence is added to consent taking in the antenatal period.

Like any other, this procedure has its own set of complications and risks. Furthermore, in its extreme it may lead to serious morbidity and even death in the rarest of circumstances. The procedure is so common that any clinician may expect her or his share of serious complications. If the patient has been forewarned it is easily handled, but if she feels that the explanation was insufficient, it opens the door for litigation.

An episiotomy performed without adequate consent is a serious offence and is an act which could lead to the possibility of an action for heavy damages against those involved. This procedure not only presents risks to maternal health, but also fetal health and has increased risks to the medical staff as well as to the attendants.

Commonly documented problems of episiotomy
- Haemorrhage (severe possible)   10%
- Wound breakdown (infection)
- Fatal infectious complication in necrotising fasciitis
- Chronic dyspareunia and sexual dysfunction
- Long-term perineal pain
- Haematoma (perineal, vulvar, vaginal, or ischiorectal)
- Anal sphincter damage
- Poor wound healing
- Long-term morbidity of anal sphincter damage (anal incontinence)
- Psychosocial consequences
- Increase in third- and fourth-degree lacerations involving the rectal sphincter
- Post-operative pain

Convalescence: An episiotomy usually heals without complications. Normal activities can be resumed shortly after birth. Proper hygiene and avoidance of constipation is advised (if possible). Pain and discomfort can be relieved with warm baths and medications.[4]

Blood loss: There is on average an increase of 300 cc or more for about 10% of women undergoing episiotomy. Simple avoidance of episiotomy may be the most powerful means to prevent excessive intrapartum haemorrhage. Restrictive use of episiotomy results in a lower risk of clinical morbidity.

Morbidity of anal sphincter damage: The long-term morbidity of the anal sphincter damage induced by episiotomy, particularly midline, has generally been underestimated in both its frequency and severity. It used to be a common belief that proper care of third-degree extensions of midline episiotomies would prevent long-term morbidity.

Sultan et al[4] found that 47% of women with third-degree tears remained symptomatic 6 to 21 months after delivery, with anal incontinence (mostly to flatus, a few to liquid stool) and/or faecal urgency, compared with only 13% of controls. Ultrasonography revealed internal and/or external anal sphincter defects in 85% of women with third-degree lacerations, in all of the symptomatic ones, and in 33% of controls.

However, the same team found an association between performance of a medio-lateral episiotomy and the development of occult sphincter defects only in univariate analysis; it disappeared as a significant factor in subsequent logistic regression analysis.

Psychosocial consequences: Although psychosocial morbidity is obviously more difficult to quantify, such effects are nevertheless both valid and important outcomes of our interventions. Use of any of several intrapartum interventions including episiotomy is negatively correlated with the patient's overall satisfaction with the birth experience. About 20% of women feel 'disfigured' by the procedure.

Other rare, potential fetal and maternal complications are outlined below.

Fetal risks:
- eyelid laceration
- castration (breech birth)
- methaemoglobinemia
- lidocaine toxicity
- increased rate of vertical transmission of HIV, at least in facilities where its use is not routine.

Maternal risks:
Episiotomy may interfere with resumption and enjoyment of intercourse, both short-term and long-term. Other risks are:
- extreme fear of subsequent delivery
- intractable rectal haemorrhage
- massive vulvar haematoma
- narcotising fasciitis, myonecrosis
- relapsing toxic shock syndrome
- brain abscess, seeded from an infected episiotomy site
- hypersensitivity reactions, including anaphylactic shock, from latex contact during episiotomy repair
- endometriosis arising in the episiotomy site
- granular cell tumour of the vulva in the episiotomy scar
- clear cell carcinoma arising in the episiotomy site
- the episiotomy scar can become a site for metastasis of carcinomas, particularly of the cervix.

Risks to birth attendants: Although not strictly a part of the risk-benefit analysis for the patient, it may be profitable briefly to mention risks assumed by practitioners in performing episiotomies. Repair of a laceration or an episiotomy increases the risk of a glove perforation, usually by the suturing needle. Liberal use of episiotomy increases the operator's exposure to blood-borne pathogens.

Legal risks: Consent for a patient presenting to the hospital for maternity care does not imply episiotomy. "An episiotomy performed without adequate consent is a serious offence and is an act, which could open up the possibility of an action for heavy damages against those involved."[5]

Part 3: Complications of Instrumental Delivery

Ventouse Delivery

Vacuum extraction is one of those procedures that may seem simpler in the beginning and lead to a sense of complacency but invariably result in greater degrees of complications.[6] While maintaining adequate speed, it is important that care is taken and that the mother is properly informed about all aspects of this procedure, the risks and benefits of vacuum delivery. Deficient knowledge and incorrect technique contributes to increases in complications of instrumental delivery.

The process is easy to explain and patients usually understand it. It is important to ensure that the patient understands what may be a complicated operation and there are complications, some of which commonly occur.

Maternal complications
- Perineal laceration (third/fourth degree)   10–40%
- Vaginal wall laceration   10–16%
- Episiotomy extension   14%
- Perineal pain   5%
- Postpartum haemorrhage   25%
- Anal sphincter dysfunction/voiding dysfunction

Fetal complications
- Fetal injury and death   0.1–3/1000
- Fetal scalp injuries (superficial necrosis/widespread sloughing)
- Intracranial haemorrhage   1 in 850
- Subaponeurotic haemorrhage   1%
- Cephalohaematoma   1–26%
  (average 12.8%)
- Scalp laceration, bruising   5.5–6.5%
- Subgaleal haemorrhage   1–3.8%
- Retinal haemorrhage   17–38 %
- Lateral rectus palsy (eye)   3.25%
- Facial nerve palsy   0.46%
- Neonatal jaundice   15%
- Chignon/cup marking on face
  (all cases of vacuum-assisted delivery)

Others
- Shoulder dystocia
- Erb's palsy
- Injury to 6 and 7th cranial nerve
- Fetal death
- Instrument failure

Vaginal laceration from the entrapment of vaginal mucosa between the suction cup and fetal head is not uncommon. This can be avoided by digital examination of the entire circumference of the suction cup before initiation of vacuum extraction.

Fetal scalp injuries, subaponeurotic haemorrhage and scalp laceration occurs from prolonged application and traction and use of rigid vacuum extractor cups.[8]

Forceps Delivery

What follows for vacuum extraction mostly also follows for forceps, with there being certain similarities in the time, the place and the manner in which they are used. So, a practitioner who follows the important dictum that the patient must understand what she is going to undergo has undertaken the consent part of it well.

Complications rate and severity is greater in forceps delivery than in ventouse as the forceps blade requires more space round the fetal head and pelvic cavity. Failure of instruments is less likely than with ventouse.[9]

Maternal complications

Early
- Laceration to cervix, vagina, perineum, bladder and rectum (rare)   1 in 5
- Third degree and complete perineal tear   8–12 in 100
- Extension of episiotomies
- Haematoma
- Intrapartum rupture of unscarred uterus
- Anaesthetic complications
- Postpartum haemorrhage   25%
- Anal sphincter dysfunction/Voiding dysfunction

Late
- Urinary stress incontinence
- Faecal incontinence
- Anal sphincter injury
- Pelvic organ prolapsed

Fetal complications
- Transient facial forceps marks
- Bruising
- Facial laceration   1.0%
- Cerebral nerve palsy   0.5%
- Cephalohaematoma
- Skull fractures
- Intracranial haemorrhage   1:664
- Intracranial haemorrhage with falx or tentorial laceration
- Breathing problems
- Low Apgar score
- Cerebellar palsy, mental retardation and behavioural problems
- Damage to facial nerve   4.5 per 1000

Maternal complications range from mild or moderate to severe laceration of soft tissue. Most commonly injured are the vagina, cervix and uterus. Injury to the bladder and rectum is very rare. Late complications are related mainly to injury to the pelvic support tissues and organs.

Fetal complications can cause bruising to the face, serious injuries to the fetal scalp, brain and cranium. Cerebellar palsy, mental retardation, and behavioural problems tend to be related to hypoxic episodes or other intrapartum environmental or congenital factors.

Sequelae of instrumental delivery have found no differences among children delivered by either ventouse or forceps.[10] The use of ventouse is associated with a higher risk of failure, more cephalohaematoma and retinal haemorrhage, but less anaesthesia is used and there's also a decreased risk of a perineal and vaginal trauma.[11]

Extra procedures which may become necessary during the procedure are:[12]
- episiotomy (5–6 in 10 for vacuum assisted delivery, 9 in 10 for forceps)
- manoeuvres for shoulder dystocia
- caesarean section
- blood transfusion
- repair of perineal tear
- manual rotation prior to forceps or vacuum-assisted delivery.

Higher rates of failure and serious or frequent complications are associated with:
- higher maternal body mass index
- ultrasound estimated fetal weight greater than 4000 g or clinically large baby
- occipitoposterior position
- midcavity delivery or when 1/5 of fetal head is palpable abdominally.

Part 4: Consent Issues and Complications of Caesarean Delivery

The caesarean section is one of the most commonly performed operations in the world. It can be broadly classified into emergency and elective caesarean sections.

The elective caesarean section is in effect gynaecological surgery as far as the issues involved in obtaining the consent. There is sufficient time to explain the indication, complications and any other problems associated with procedures. The woman has adequate time to clear doubts in her mind by asking appropriate questions.

The emergency caesarean section is one of the greatest challenges to a practitioner. During an emergency situation there is not enough time to explain the situation and obtain informed consent. There is sufficient time to give only a synopsis, which suffices for most of the patient's requirements.

The problem occurs when in the physician's view a woman needs to deliver urgently due to an increased risk to her or to her unborn child's health, and she refuses to have a caesarean section. This poses the greatest challenge to the attending obstetrician, as the woman may fully understand the need for urgent delivery.

In these circumstances the time available is insufficient for the purposes of full discussion and obtaining informed consent. This can lead to extreme frustration among both parties. How best to convince a mother and at the same time ensuring her full and complete understanding of the problem remains an issue that can flummox even a very experienced health professional. In these cases, individual strategies, prior contact with the patient and a good rapport during her earlier visits is what helps the most. The patient must be willing to listen to the obstetrician and at the same time maintain her own independence in the decision-making process. Women who are obese, who have significant pathology, who have had previous surgery or who have pre-existing medical conditions must understand that the quoted risks for serious or frequent complications will be increased.

The decision for sterilisation should not be made while the woman is in labour or immediately prior to the procedure. An additional specific consent form should be used for sterilisation at caesarean section.

Some of the complications can be minimised by the use of prophylactic antibiotics and thromboprophylaxis. Complication rates from caesarean sections performed during labour are greater overall than those during planned procedures (24 % vs. 16%). Complication rates are higher at 9–10 cm dilatation than 0–1 cm dilation (33% vs. 17%).[13]

Operative complications are outlined below.[14, 15, 16, 17]

Common operative complications
- Lacerations of lower uterine segment
  (depending on urgency and stage of labour)
Vaginal lacerations	overall 1.2%
Cervical lacerations	overall 3.6%
- Haemorrhage >1000 ml   9.2%
- Hematoma
- Blood transfusion   1%
- Readmission to hospital   5%
- Infection   6%
  Wound infection
  Endometritis   6%
- UTI   6%
- Febrile morbidity   15–30%
- Elective repeat LSCS   25%
- Ectopic pregnancy
- Anaesthetic complications

Rare complications
- Re-operation
- Thromboembolism   2–4 fold
                             compared with
                             vaginal birth
- DVT
- PE
- Need for further surgery
- Hysterectomy   0.2%
- Bladder injury   0.1%
- Uteral injury   0.03%
- Bowel injury   extremely rare
- Small bowel obstruction   5 per 1000

- Severe acute maternal morbidity   2.5 times to
                                                6 times
- Maternal mortality   1 in 12,000
- DIC
- Serious infectious morbidity (defined as bacteremia, septic shock, septic thrombophlebitis, necrotizing fasciitis or death attributed to infection)   1–2%
- Relative risk for emergency CS compared   1.7:1
  with elective

Uterine rupture in future pregnancy
- After myomectomy scar   0.02%
- After 1 CS   0.5–1%
- After classical section   6–12%
- Two prior CS   1.8–3.7%
- Uterine dehiscence   9%
- Placenta praevia and placenta accreta   0.4–0.8%
- Long-term subfertility is recognised problem

Fetal complications
- Low Apgar score
- Breathing problem in newborn
- Intracranial haemorrhage
- Fetal lacerations   1–2%

No. of CS[18, 19]	Incidence of placenta accreta	Incidence of placenta accreta in women with previa	% of women needing hysterectomy	Incidence of placenta previa
1	0.24%	3.3%	0.65%	1.86%
2	0.31%	11%	0.42%	5.49%
3	0.57%	40%	0.90%	14.28%
4	2.13%	61%	2.41%	
5	2.33%	67%	3.49%	
6	6.74%	67%	8.99%	

Table 1: Comparison of complication rates related to number of CS

Post caesarean endometritis is defined as a persistent fever of 100.4°F beyond 24 hours after delivery. Treatment consists of gentamycin plus clindamycin and ampicillin (or vancomycin). Treatment is considered to be failed if fever persists after 5 days of antibiotics and 72 hours of triple antibiotics. 54% of patients recover after 48 hours and almost 94% at 76 hours. If the temperature does not come down then the possibility of wound infection, wound abscess, or intraperitoneal collection should be suspected.

Imaging techniques such as ultrasound scan, CT scan or MRI should be performed to localise the intraperitoneal collection of pus. Further attempts to detect pelvic and ovarian vein thrombosis should be made in patients where diagnosis is not clear, and they should be treated with heparin.[20]

Risk factors for complications include:
- excessive speed
- lack of practitioner experience
- previous CS
- gestational age <32 weeks
- low station of presenting parts
- ruptured membranes preoperatively.

Other factors include:
- previous pelvic surgery
- bowel surgery for inflammatory bowel disease.

Part 5: Complications of the Induction of Labour

Induction of labour refers to the iatrogenic stimulation of uterine contraction prior to the onset of spontaneous labour. This is one of the most commonly performed obstetrical procedures. Induction of labour is indicated where there is increased risk to the mother and the baby by conserving the pregnancy. The induction rate varies from institution to institution and in 2008–2009, 20.2% of all deliveries in the UK were induced.[21]

Complication and failure rate increases in cases of an unfavourable cervix. All methods carry risks. The various PGE2 preparations have up to a 5% rate of hyperstimulation (excessive painful contractions).

Complications
- Failure to induce effective contraction
- Placental separation (accidental haemorrhage)
- Postpartum bleeding
- Fetal hypoxia
- Pulmonary embolism (amniotic fluid embolism)
- Poor uterine action – incoordinate uterine action/dysfunctional labour
- Chorioamnionitis
- Induction after CS scar   2–3 fold increase in LSCS

- Cord prolapse
- Hyperstimulation
- Precipitate labour
- Uterine rupture
- Hyponatremia
- Hypotension

Before determining failed induction adequate time should be allowed (12 and 16 hours in multi and primigravida respectively).

Risks associated with amniotomy include the introduction of infection, disruption of occult placenta praevia, rupture of vasa praevia and umbilical cord prolapse. The laminaria tent and hygroscopic dilator has a higher incidence of postpartum maternal and fetal infections.

Meconium aspiration is common in women induced with misoprostol with no different outcome.

Antidiuretic effects of oxytocin in high doses can cause water intoxication (prolonged and increased dose of syntocinon causes retention of large amounts of electrolyte-free fluid). This can cause headache, anorexia, nausea, vomiting, abdominal pain, lethargy, drowsiness, unconsciousness, grand mal type seizures and potentially irreversible neurologic injury.

Incidence of uterine rupture during induced trials of labour with a previous CS delivery depends on many factors. The overall rate of uterine rupture is 15/2119 (0.71%). The uterine rupture rate with induced TOL (8/575, 1.4%) is significantly higher than with spontaneous TOL (7/1544, 0.45%), p=0.036. The relative risk of uterine rupture with induction is 3.09 (95% CI 1.12 to 8.42). Uterine rupture rates by method of induction (alone or in combination with another) are shown in the table below and are compared with uterine rupture during spontaneous TOL.

Induction Method	Rupture Rate
PGE2	2.9%
ARM	1.5%
Oxytocin	1.2%
Spontaneous TOL	0.45%

Table 2: Rupture rates of different induction methods

The overall rate of rupture among all patients with induction of labour was 2.3%, in comparison with 0.7% among women with spontaneous labour. Acceleration with oxytocin uterine rupture was 2.3 times more likely, and with the use of prostaglandin E2 gel, rupture was 3.2 times more likely.[22, 23]

Part 6: Complications due to Invasive Prenatal Diagnostic Tests

Amniocentesis

Although the risk of the procedure is low, the complications of this test are important.

Complications
- Lower chance of normal delivery
- Increased risk related to amniotic fluid and membrane
- Hypotonic uterine dysfunction
- Talipes equinovarus and congenital hip dislocation occurs in early amniocentesis
- Amniotic fluid leakage   1.7%
- Pregnancy loss   0.5%–1%
- Feto-maternal haemorrhage (Rh isoimmunisation)
- Infection (chorioamnionitis)
- Respiratory disorder in infancy (RDS and pneumonia)   1.1%
- Abdominal pain   8%
- Fetal damage is infrequent (cardiac tamponade, ocular trauma, gangrene of fetal limb)
- Contamination of amniotic fluid sample with maternal blood cells

---

	Amniocentesis	CVS
Miscarriage	2.70%	4.17%
One puncture	4.76%	3.75%
Two punctures		N/A
Preterm loss <32 weeks		16.6%
Preterm loss <35 weeks		23.8%
Fetal loss		10.2%
Fetal loss after feticide		8.3%

Table 3: Risk of loss in twin pregnancy in amniocentesis and CVS[24]

Risks were higher if done before 15 weeks. There were 10 fold increases in monoamniotic twins after CVS. Fetal structural defect was higher in CVS and early amniocentesis.[25]

Chorionic Villous Biopsy

After chorionic villous biopsy, the risk of miscarriage is increased by 1% for the remainder of the pregnancy. 50% of miscarriage occurs within the first 2 weeks after the test. Cramping may occur during chorionic villous biopsy and for a short while afterwards. Infection is very rare and usually occurs within 24 to 72 hours after the chorionic villous biopsy.

Repeat testing is needed rarely, due to an inability to obtain sufficient placental tissue or if the laboratory test fails to give a result.

Injury to the baby is extremely rare. If the procedure is carried out before 10 weeks there is a small risk to the growth of the baby's arms or legs. This is not found where the testing has occurred after 10 weeks. Care is taken to place the needle only in the placenta.

Immediate risks
- Cramping
- Failure or repeated needling
- Insufficient sample   <2%
- Placental mosaicism   1% to 3%

Later risks
- Miscarriage
- Infection
- Injury to baby
- Culture failure

Potential long-term complications
- Rh isoimmunization
- Prematurity
- Placental abnormalities
- Birth defects
- There may be increased incidence of delayed rupture of membrane

---

There may be an increased incidence of delayed membrane damage. There have been several reports of oligohydramnios detected at 16 to 20 weeks in patients who have had CVS. Almost all had a history of persistent vaginal spotting or wetness after the procedure. No information exists to suggest that fetal growth is affected by CVS.

A sufficient sample for diagnosis is obtained in 98% of the procedures performed. Culture failure occurs in less than 1% of cases. Immediate rupture of fetal membranes is extremely uncommon.

An overall spontaneous abortion rate of 3.5–4% has been cited, but no control data on the background risk for patients of similar maternal and gestational age are available. Risks related to the procedure may be 1% or less. Preliminary data from an NIH collaborative study indicated that CVS has a 0.7% higher pregnancy loss rate than amniocentesis.

Maternal cell contamination has been a source of several diagnostic errors; the occurrence appears to be related to the experience of the operator.

A potential source of error that is more difficult to control is the existence of discrepancies between the chromosomal constitution of the fetus and that of the chorionic villi. These discrepancies may be in the form of chromosomal aneuploidy confined only to the villus sample and appear to represent true mosaicism within the placenta. The incidence of this finding has ranged from 1% to 2%. Although the significance of placental mosaicism is unknown, it may be associated with increased risk of pregnancy loss. In such cases, amniocentesis should be offered for confirmation.[26]

Fetal Blood Sampling

Fetal blood sampling is performed by specially trained perinatologists as part of diagnosing, treating, and monitoring fetal problems at various times during pregnancy. Fetal blood PH correctly predicts neonatal outcomes 82% of the time, as measured by the Apgar score. The false positive rate is about 8% and false negative rate about 10%. PO2 and PCO2 do not correlate as well with the Apgar score as does PH.

Complications
- Infection
- Continued bleeding from the fetal sampling site
- Fetal scalp bruising
- Changes in the fetal heart rate
- Transmission of infection such as HIV, herpes and streptococcus
- Abscess formation
- Amniotic fluid contamination (may lead to inaccurate PH)
- Leaking of amniotic fluid
- Fetal death

Part 7: Cervical Cerclage

Cerclage should be delayed until after 14 weeks so that early miscarriage due to other factors will be possible. There is no consensus as to how late in pregnancy the procedure should be performed. However, an emergency measure after the cervix is effaced can be done as late as the 26th week, but is rarely used after 24 weeks. The later in pregnancy, the more likely surgical intervention will stimulate preterm labour (SROM). Ultrasound is done to assure a live fetus and to exclude major fetal anomalies. Infection, bleeding or contractions are contraindications to cerclage. Abstinence from intercourse/orgasm is recommended for one week before and one week after the procedure. Aerobic exercise is contraindicated, although walking and isometric exercise is allowed.

Complications
- Bleeding
- Ruptured membranes
- Failure   20%
- Preterm labour
- Chorioamnionitis
- Cervical stenosis
- Damage to cervix during surgery
- Cervical tear if suture not removed in time
- Cervical infection (fever, chill, smelly discharge) before and after childbirth
- Risks associated with anaesthesia

Cerclage does not prevent all preterm deliveries. A study in the September 2003 issue of *Obstetrics & Gynecology*[27] found that the use of cervical cerclage is not effective in preventing preterm birth or miscarriage in women at moderate risk of preterm birth or second trimester pregnancy loss.

Controversies

1. The role of antibiotics, tocolytics, and progestins.

2. Option of trans-abdominal cerclage.
There is no evidence that TAC is superior to transvaginal cerclage as an initial procedure. TAC is associated with far more morbidity than transvaginal cerclage. It requires a laparotomy for placement and

subsequent caesarean delivery is necessary. For these reasons, TAC should be reserved for patients with documented cervical incompetence who have either failed previous transvaginal cerclage or in whom a transvaginal cerclage is technically impossible.

3. Necessary follow-up after placement.

4. Optimal time for removal.
Removal before 36 weeks should be avoided, beyond 38 weeks the benefits are negligible.

5. Removal of cerclage after membrane rupture.

6. Placement of a cerclage in a woman with a short cervix.
A patient with a history of prior idiopathic preterm delivery who is found via ultrasound to have a shortened cervix may benefit from early cerclage placement.

7. Prophylactic cerclage in DES-exposed women.
Prophylactic cerclage is not indicated in patients with a history of in utero exposure to DES unless those women have experienced a previous pregnancy loss or there is clear evidence of cervical shortening. One reason is the fact that the DES-exposed cervix responds differently to surgery. Further studies are required to clarify this issue.

8. What is the role of cervical cerclage in multiple gestations?

9. Should a cerclage be placed prior to pregnancy?

10. Is there a role for permanent cerclage placement?
Although it has become the basic management tool for cervical incompetence especially in an emergency, cerclage remains a procedure with well-defined risks and questionable benefits. Thus, it should be used judiciously.

Part 8: Complications of External Cephalic Version (ECV)

Reports from published studies indicate that there are fewer caesarean deliveries among women who have undergone successful version compared with women who have not undergone ECV. One randomised trial found no significant difference between the caesarean delivery rates with an ECV attempt and controls that did not undergo ECV. The success rate improved with gestational age, with increasing parity, with increasing age of the mother and her increasing body weight. Success rate is 30–80%. The location of the placenta did not play a decisive role. The success rate of the version was remarkably good, even in cases with small-for-gestational age fetuses and large-for-gestational age fetuses as well as in cases with a previous caesarean section. ECV is rarely associated with complications.[28, 29]

Complications	
• Incidence of CS during ECV	0.5%
• Risk of spontaneous reversion	7%
• Placental abruption	
• Preterm labour	
• Rupture of membrane with cord prolapsed	
• Risk of feto-maternal haemorrhage	
• Uterine rupture in extreme circumstances	
• Perinatal loss	1% (approx)

Fetal heart rate changes during attempted versions are not uncommon but it usually stabilises when the procedure is discontinued. Serious adverse effects associated with ECV do not occur often, but there have been a few reported cases of intrauterine death, and premature partial separation of the placenta.

Although the incidence of serious complications associated with ECV is low, the potential is present, making it prudent to perform ECV in a facility that has ready access to caesarean delivery services.

Part 9: Complications of Anti-D

RhD alloimmunisation still occurs. However, the most important cause of anti-D antibodies is now immunisation during pregnancy where there has been no overt sensitising event. Late immunisation during the third trimester of a first pregnancy is responsible for 18–27% of cases. Routine use of antenatal anti-D (500 iu) is recommended at 28 and 34 weeks of gestation to all non-sensitised women (RhD-negative).

The attending clinician should discuss and clearly explain to the patient routine antenatal anti-D and postnatal prophylaxis and its side effects. Women who are eligible for this should receive written information before making an informed decision about opting for treatment.

Consent should be obtained and recorded in the case notes of the patient. In the absence of RAADP, approximately 1% of RhD-negative women who deliver an RhD-positive baby will become sensitized. No serious adverse events were reported in the clinical studies reviewed in the 2009 Health Technology Assessment. Information from manufacturers indicates a very low rate of adverse event reporting (<1/85,000 doses), with only a minority of these classified as serious and possibly related to treatment.[30]

Complications
- Cost
- Pain
- Itching, redness at the injection site
- Hypersensitivity reaction
- Maternal death

Short-term discomfort at the injection site and anaphylactic reaction may occur in patients who have antibodies to IgA, or patients who have had an atypical reaction to blood transfusion or treatment with plasma derivatives.

The healthcare professional should discuss the situations where anti-D prophylaxis would be neither necessary nor cost effective such as if the woman:
- has opted to be sterilised
- is in a stable relationship with the father of the child, who is RhD-negative
- is certain that she will not have another child.

Part 10: Postnatal Consent and Complications of Immunisation for Neonates

BCG Immunisation

Neonatal BCG should be offered only to the infants at increased risk such as those who:

- live in a house with a person who has either a current or past history of tuberculosis
- has one or both parents who identify as Pacific People
- has household members who have lived in the last five years in countries where there is a high incidence of TB
- during their first five years will be living for three months or longer in a high incidence country.

BCG vaccination criteria should be discussed with the parent and a BCG consent form should be signed by parent.

Immediate	Late	Rare
Vasovagal attack	Localised abscess formation	Axillary lymphadenitis
Anaphylaxis (extremely rare): May cause redness of the face and neck, swelling of the face, throat or neck, skin rash, and breathing difficulties	Prominent lymphadenopathy	Lupoid and other skin disorders
Localised erythematous rash at injection site	Keloid scars at injection site	Osteitis
Low grade fever (for first 24 hours)		Osteomyelitis
		Neurological disorders

Table 4: Complications following BCG immunisation

Hepatitis B Immunisation

Hepatitis vaccine is recommended for all newborn babies. All pregnant women should be tested for hepatitis B early in their pregnancy. If it is positive the baby should also receive hepatitis B immunoglobulin. If the recommended immunisations are completed the baby's risk of becoming infected is reduced by about 95%.

Parents should sign their consent in two places on the National Hepatitis B Immunisation form if hepatitis B positive. If hepatitis B status is unknown then consent for hepatitis B vaccine only is required.

Complications
- Injection site reactions contribute almost a quarter of all adverse effects
- Temporary pain at injection site (common)   3–9%
- Mild to moderate fever   4–7%
- Soreness, redness and swelling at injection site
- A low rate of anaphylaxis (hives, difficulty breathing, shock)
- Rare report of hair loss

Any presumed evidence of adverse events must be weighed against the very strong evidence that the vaccine has in protecting against HBV-related liver disease and death. There is no confirmed scientific evidence for chronic illnesses including multiple sclerosis, chronic fatigue syndrome, rheumatoid arthritis or autoimmune disorders.[31]

Vitamin K to Newborns

Haemorrhagic diseases of the newborn can be prevented by administration of vitamin K to the newborn. Giving 1 mg of vitamin K intramuscularly at the time of birth prevents the fall in vitamin K dependent factors in full term infants. Although oral vitamin K has been suggested as an alternative it is not universally accepted. Several oral doses are essential to give enough protection as vitamin K is not absorbed. When given by mouth its effect does not last as long. Therefore, it should be given to all newborns as a single IM injection.

Complications
- Injections create avenues of infection for newborn
- Possible trauma from injections can jeopardise the establishment of breastfeeding
- Higher clotting factors may increase risk from bacterial infections

Concern regarding a possible causal association between parental vitamin K and childhood cancer has not been substantiated.

Informed consent should be taken from the parent before administration of vitamin K to the newborn.

Part 11: Intrauterine Fetal Death

IUFD is fetal death after 24 weeks gestation but before the onset of labour. It complicates about 0.5% of pregnancies. With the development of diagnostic and therapeutic modalities, the management of IUD had shifted from watchful expectancy to more active interventions.[32, 33]

A Swedish study had showed that an interval of 24 hours or more from the diagnosis of death in utero to the start of labour was associated with an increased risk of moderately severe anxiety or worse.[34] Vaginal birth can be achieved within 24 hours of induction of labour for IUFD in about 90% of cases.[35]

Complications
- Psychological trauma to the patient
- Operative procedure during delivery
- Forceps   1.6%
- Caesarean section   4.8%
- Cervical and perineal laceration   9.4%
- Endometritis   12%
- Maternal death   0.2%
- Uterine dehiscence
- Uterine rupture
- HELLP syndrome
  (Haemolysis, Elevated Liver enzyme, Low Platelet)
- DIC

Part 12: How to Reduce Legal Risk in Shoulder Dystocia

Shoulder dystocia is a rare event and seldom results in permanent injury to the newborn. Unfortunately, shoulder dystocia is not predictable and cannot be prevented by performing caesarean section. 50% of shoulder dystocia occurs in patients without having any risk factors. Therefore, performing more caesareans will not have a substantial impact on preventing injuries (it can occur during caesarean deliveries as well).

There would need to be a large number of caesarean deliveries required to prevent a single shoulder dystocia. Medico-legal systems operate in such a way that they try to assign blame in order for financial assistance to be given to the unfortunate newborn that may be affected by these complications. Therefore, it is important to thoroughly document all the steps and care given to the patient antenatally and during labour.

Shoulder dystocia and brachial palsy are the most common lawsuits against obstetricians for medical malpractice. The vast majority of shoulder dystocia is unpredictable and presents as an acute medical emergency.

Documentation of delivery is central to reducing liability. The attending doctor should write an accurate and honest delivery note. If a trainee doctor is involved in the procedure, they should also write a delivery note and indicate how the trainer or senior doctor provided the supervision.[36]

The delivery note should include the following:
- position of the fetal head
- which shoulder was the anterior shoulder
- time of delivery of fetal head
- time of delivery of fetal body
- staff present (midwife, obstetrician, paediatrician, anaesthetist)
- manoeuvres used to achieve delivery
- newborn weight and Apgar score
- cord blood gas
- any deficit of motion of the extremities
- disposition of the newborn
- any maternal injuries (perineal lacerations, postpartum haemorrhage).

Part 13: Placental Removal

Complications of manual removal of placenta
- Bleeding
- Infection
- Inversion
- Broad ligament haematoma
- Need for hysterectomy
- Perforation resulting in trauma to pelvic organs
  (including bowel, bladder, ureters, nerves, and vessels)
- Incomplete removal
  (especially in cases of placenta accreta/increta)

Manual removal of the placenta is a common procedure requiring expertise to avoid serious complications. Strict protocols and guidelines should be followed.

Part 14: Neurologic Injury Associated with Pregnancy and Delivery

Neurological and Anaesthetic Complications

Complication	Usual Cause	Sensory Deficit	Motor Deficit
Prolapsed disc	Spontaneous occurrence in 1:6000 deliveries	Variable	Variable
Lumbosacral trunk L4, L5	Compression of head against sacrum, higher incidence with use of forceps	Hypoaesthesia lateral calf and foot	Weak hip adductor foot drop weak quadriceps
Lateral femoral cutaneous L2, L3	Lithotomy or retractors	Numbness anterolateral thigh	
Sciatic nerve L4, L5, S1, S2, S3	Lithotomy or IM injection	Pain from posterior gluteal to foot	Inability to flex leg
Obturator nerve L2, L3, L4	Lithotomy, acute flexion of thigh	Hypoesthesia medial thigh	Inability to adduct leg
Common peroneal L4, L5, S1, S2	Lithotomy with compression of the lateral aspect of the knee	Anterolateral calf and dorsum of foot and toes	Plantar flexion with inversion deformity – foot drop
Saphenous nerve L2, L3, L4	Lithotomy position	Medial foot and anteromedial aspect lower leg	

Table 5: Neurologic injury associated with pregnancy and delivery

Neurological complications in obstetric patients must be divided into 1) obstetrical causes, and 2) anaesthesia-related causes.[37, 38, 39]

The incidence of neurological complications related to obstetric causes varies from 1:2600 to 1:6400. These neurological complications are associated with prolonged labour and forceps delivery.

Changes in obstetric practice of difficult deliveries have decreased the incidence of major obstetrical-related neurological complications. Peripheral nerves which might be involved but are unrelated to regional anaesthesia include prolapsed intervertebral discs relating to the exertion of labour causing spinal root compression. The incidence has been documented as 1 in 6000 deliveries.

The lumbosacral trunk (L4, L5) may be compressed between the descending fetal head and the ala of the sacrum. It might be associated with the use of mid to high forceps. Clinical findings may include foot drop, hypoesthesia of the lateral foot and calf, slight weakness of hip adductors, and quadriceps weakness.

Neurological complications can occur in the lithotomy position from hyperacute hip flexion, as well as due to retractors during CS. There will be impaired knee extension due to quadriceps paralysis, absence of the patellar reflex and hypoesthesia of the anterior thigh and medial aspect of the calf.

The lateral femoral cutaneous nerve (L2, L3) can be injured by retractors during caesarean section, or during incorrect lithotomy positioning. There will be transient numbness of the thigh at the anterolateral aspect.

The sciatic nerve (L4, L5 and S1, S2, S3) can be injured with incorrect lithotomy positioning with knee extension and external hip rotation. There will be pain in the gluteal region radiating to the foot, inability of the flexion of the leg.

The obturator nerve (L2, L3, L4) may be injured due to lithotomy positioning. Acute flexion in the thigh to groin area, particularly in the obese patient, may lead to compression causing weakness or paralysis of the thigh abductors.

The common peroneal nerve (L4, L5, S1, S2) may be involved in pressure injury with lithotomy positioning due to prolonged compression of the lateral aspect of the knee. The patient will lose the ability to assume an erect position. There will be associated foot drop.

The saphenous nerve (L2, L3, L4) can be affected during lithotomy positioning. There will be loss of sensation over the medial aspect of the foot and anteromedial aspect of the lower leg.

Part 15: Complications of Spinal Anaesthesia

Very common and common side effects
(these may be unpleasant but are easily treatable)
- Spinal tap   3.2–7.6%
- Spinal anaesthetic extending to high level
- Injection of anaesthetic agent into a vein
- Hypotension   1.4%
- High rate of instrumental delivery
- Loss of bearing down sensation
- Post delivery retention of urine
- Post-operative headache   1–3%
                                                                   (25 gauge needle)

- Urinary retention
- Failure/inadequate analgesia
- Itching
- Pain during the injection
- Hypotension/bradycardia/cardiac arrest
- Nausea, vomiting
- Extensive spread of spinal anaesthesia
- Backache   19%
- Neurological sequelae (headache)   2–5%

Rare complications
- Serious complications   0.45:10,000
- Nerve damage/paraplegia
- Permanent cauda equina syndrome
- Peroneal nerve paresis/neurological deficit

The main complication that may arise from the incorrect insertion of a catheter into the epidural space is a spinal tap. The frequency of dural tap clearly depends on experience. The frequency and severity of hypotensive episodes depends on many factors including the correct positioning of the patients, preloading of fluid etc. The effect of the epidural block on the levator ani and perineal sensation has important implications for the second stage. Sometimes it can be difficult to find the dural space and impossible to obtain CSF.

Hypotension may occur with higher blocks.

There is a theoretical risk of introducing infection into the sub-arachnoid space and causing meningitis. This should never happen if equipment is sterilised properly and an aseptic technique is used.

A characteristic headache may occur within a few hours and can last a week or more. It is postural, worsened by standing or even raising the head and is relieved by lying down. It is more common in the young, especially in obstetric patients. It is thought to be caused by the continuing loss of CSF through the hole made in the dura by the spinal needle.

Urinary retention may occur as the sacral autonomic fibres are among the last to recover following a spinal anaesthetic.

Injection of inappropriate drugs into the CSF can produce meningitis, arachnoiditis, transverse myelitis or the cauda equina syndrome with varying patterns of neurological impairment and sphincter disturbances. Damage to an epidural vein can lead to the formation of an epidural haematoma that compresses the spinal cord.

Nerve damage is a rare complication of spinal anaesthesia. Temporary loss of sensation, pins and needles and sometimes muscle weakness may last for a few days or even weeks but almost all of these make a full recovery in time.

Itching can occur as a side effect of using morphine-like drugs in combination with local anaesthetic.

The advantages of spinal anaesthesia are:
• quick onset
• technically easier to perform than other types of anaesthesia.

Part 16: Complications Associated with Epidural Anaesthesia

Fortunately incidences of serious complication with epidural anaesthesia are rare in experienced hands. However, they do occur, even with the most experienced and good intentioned practitioner.

Direct trauma to the spinal cord after an epidural anaesthesia for labour would be very rare, as the epidural space is usually entered below the conus medullaris.

Incidence of serious complications	0.52:10,000
• Nerve damage	
• Nerve root trauma	0.07%
• Paraparesis	
• Paresthesia	5–25%
• Permanent cauda equina syndrome	
• Peroneal nerve paresis	
• Neurological deficit	
• Brain damage	
• Motor deficit	0–15%
• Bacterial infection	
• Acute toxic reactions	
• Headache	76–85%
• Neonatal death	
• Pain during anaesthesia	
• Emotional distress	
• Back pain	30–40%
• Accidental dural puncture	1–2%
• Bladder dysfunction	
• Shivering and shaking	
• Broken epidural catheter	

Epidural anesthesia can be associated with neurologic problems, ranging from headache to paralysis.[40, 41, 42, 43, 44] Injuries include:
- prolonged neural blockade
- backache
- trauma to nerve roots
- cauda equina syndrome
- epidural hematoma
- epidural abscess
- adhesive arachnoiditis
- meningitis
- postdural puncture headache.

Cauda equina syndrome and adhesive arachnoiditis share a common etiology (chemical toxicity as a consequence of local anaesthetic toxicity). Epidural abscess has been reported in a frequency of 1:505,000 patients who had epidurals. (The incidence is 2:10,000 in patients without regional anesthesia.)

In 90% of adults, the cord ends above the second lumbar vertebrae. However, in 10% of adults, it extends to the third lumbar vertebrae. Pain and/or paraesthesia during needle placement or injection of medication, usually warn of risk for injury and should be acted upon. (If paresthesia persists, the catheter should be removed and reinserted in another space.[45]

The actual incidence of epidural hematoma is unknown. Risk factors for epidural hematoma have included difficult or bloody tap, pre-existing coagulopathy and use of anticoagulants. The risk of a bloody tap in the obstetric population has been reported to be as high as 18%.

Overstretching of the bladder due to a prolonged continuous epidural blockade can produce this problem. Longer acting local anaesthetics are more often associated with this complication.

Patchy sensory anaesthesia and motor deficit occasionally lasts for as long as 10 to 48 hours but is ultimately resolved.

Massive epidural represents an excessive segmental spread from the relative over dosage of local anaesthetic. This problem is more often seen in very obese individuals as well as in patients with severe arteriosclerosis and diabetes. The onset of this problem is more gradual and it very rarely spreads high enough to produce unconsciousness.

Accidental intravascular injection can happen either at the time of induction of the epidural anaesthesia or result from subsequent migration of the epidural catheter in the intravascular space. Injection of local anaesthetic directly into the epidural vein can give rise to systemic reaction causing convulsions as well as possible cardiovascular collapse. Initiation of immediate management is important: left uterine displacement management of airway, if necessary by endotracheal tube and ventilation with 100% oxygen. The convulsion is usually short-lived but if it continues, one has to use 5–10 mg of diazepam or a small amount of thiopentone (50–100 mg). Fetal heart rate monitoring will ultimately govern the next step: a) if fetal heart rate is normal, labour can continue for vaginal delivery, b) in presence of fetal distress, immediate caesarean section should be planned under general anaesthesia, active resuscitation of the fetus may be necessary.

Backache is a frequent problem (30–40%) following epidural analgesia in obstetric patients. It may be related to improperly placed retractors and thus unrelated to regional anaesthesia. Multiple attempts with needles may increase back pain.

Methemoglobinemia is associated with prilocaine, especially when the dose exceeds 600 mg.

Advantages of epidurals include:
- lower incidence of hypotension
- unlimited duration
- able to use for post-op analgesia
- possibility of less motor blockade
- less risk of headache.

Part 17: Complications of General Anaesthesia

Very common and common complications
- Feeling sick and vomiting after surgery
- Sore throat
- Dizziness, blurred vision
- Shivering
- Headache
- Itching
- Aches, pains and backache
- Pain during injection of drugs
- Bruising and soreness
- Confusion or memory loss

Uncommon side effects and complications
- Chest infection
- Bladder problems
- Muscle pains
- Slow breathing (depressed respiration)
- Damage to teeth, lips or tongue
- An existing medical condition getting worse
- Awareness

Rare or very rare complications
- Damage to the eyes
- Serious allergy to drugs
- Nerve damage
- Death
- Equipment failure

Intubation tubes in airways may give a sore throat, which can last from a few hours to days.

The anaesthetic agent itself or loss of fluids may lower blood pressure and make the patient feel faint. Headaches usually get better in a few hours and can be treated with pain relievers. If they last a long time they may need special treatment.

Drugs used may cause some pain or discomfort when they are injected. This may be caused around the injection and drip sites by a thin vein bursting, movement of a nearby joint, or infection. It normally settles without treatment but if the area becomes uncomfortable the position of the drip should be changed.

A chest infection is more likely to happen in people who smoke and may lead to breathing difficulties (smoking should be avoided for as long as possible before the anaesthetic).

Certain types of operation and regional anaesthesia (particularly with a spinal or epidural), can cause difficulty in passing urine and women tend to leak. To prevent these problems a urinary catheter may be inserted at a suitable time.

Some pain-relieving drugs can cause slow breathing or drowsiness after the surgery. If muscle relaxants are still having an effect (have not been fully reversed), the breathing muscles may be weak.

Damage can be caused to teeth by clenching during recovery. Anaesthetists take great care to protect eyes and eyelids are held closed with adhesive tape, which is removed before recovery. However, sterilising fluids can leak past the tapes or eyes can get scratched while waking up after the tapes have been removed. These can cause damage to the surface of the eye.

Allergic reactions will be noticed and treated very quickly. Very rarely these reactions lead to death, even in healthy people.

Nerve damage (paralysis or numbness) may be due to the needle when performing a regional block, or it can be caused by pressure on a nerve during an operation. Most nerve damage is temporary and recovers within two to three months.

Deaths resulting from anaesthesia are very rare, and are usually caused by a combination of factors. There are probably about five deaths for every million anaesthetics given in the UK.

Vital equipment that could fail includes the anaesthetic gas supply or the ventilator. Monitors are now used which give an immediate warning of problems, and these failures rarely have serious effects.

Some operations and anaesthetic and pain-relieving drugs are more likely to cause sickness (nausea) than others. Sickness can be treated with anti-vomiting drugs (anti-emetics), but it may last from a few hours to several days.

An analysis of closed claims revealed that nerve injury is more likely with general anaesthesia than regional anaesthesia (61% vs 36%). Ulnar nerve palsy and brachial plexus injury were the most common, followed by lumbosacral nerve root injury.

Part 18: Complications of Local Anaesthesia

Allergic reactions range from rashes to severe hypersensitivity reactions, and if used in the antenatal period can cause reduced fetal heart rates. Elderly people are more prone to some of the effects.

Occasional side effects
- Sleepiness
- Dizziness
- Vertigo
- Confusion
- Blurred vision
- Trembling
- Tingling
- Temperature fluctuation
- Mood changes
- Stomach upset

Very occasional side effects
- Convulsions
- Impaired consciousness
- Shallow breathing
- Reduced blood pressure
- Low pulse rate
- Abdominal heart rate
- Shock

Part 19: Complications related to Gynaecological Procedures

Thromboembolism

The risk of clinically significant VTE in benign gynaecological surgery is rare. Prophylaxis by multiple methods does not completely eliminate this risk. Preoperative counselling is just as important to risk management as prudent prophylaxis. Incidents of VTE are less than 1:500 operations undertaken for benign disease with no previous history of VTE, or factor C laden deficiency and surgical anaesthesia lasting <3 hrs.

Type of Venous Thromboembolism	Risk
Asymptomatic DVT	25%
Asymptomatic proximal DVT	7%
Symptomatic DVT	6%
Symptomatic nonfatal PE	1–2%
Fatal PE	0.5%

Table 6: Risk of venous thromboembolism following general and gynaecological surgery in the absence of thromboprophylaxis[46]

A patient undergoing a major gynaecological procedure (of more than 30 minutes) has significant risk of venous thromboembolism. The risk is greater if additional risk factors are present. Therefore the patient should be counselled appropriately.

Neuropathy after Pelvic Surgery

Post-operative neuropathy is a well-recognised complication after pelvic surgery but it is not a frequent occurrence and those affected often make a full recovery. This most commonly occurs during the procedures undertaken for hysterectomy, endometrial or cervical cancer, ovarian cancer debulking and surgeries for various other malignant or benign conditions. Incidents of post-operative neuropathy are 1.9%. Motor deficiency improves by physiotherapy; sensory deficits or pain are treated with pharmacological or surgical management. The overall and complete recovery occurs in almost 73% and time to resolution of symptoms varies widely depending on the severity of injury.[47]

Part 20: Complications after Gynaecological Surgery

Sexual Function and Hysterectomy

Each year at least 70,000 hysterectomies are performed as a treatment for chronic or benign gynaecological conditions, although very little has been published about the hysterectomy decision-making process. Patients are concerned about effects on their sexual functioning, which is the most frequent anxiety. Sexual function overall improves after hysterectomy. The frequency of sexual activity increased, sexual satisfaction increased and problems with sexual functioning decreased. This is probably due to amelioration of the symptoms that have previously had a negative effect on sexual function.[48, 49, 50]

Bowel Obstruction after Gynaecological Surgery

Post-surgical adhesion has now become the leading cause of bowel obstruction in the Western world. The interval between the initial laparotomy and the bowel obstruction varies from 1 month to 20 years. Adhesions involving the site of pelvic reperitonealisation were responsible in 85% of cases, while adhesions to the anterior wall accounted for 15%.

Type of Operation	Women with Bowel Obstruction per 1000 Operations
Hysterectomy	16.3
Adenexal surgery	8.7
Myomectomy	3.9
Caesarean section	0.5

Table 7: Antecedent gynaecologic operations in women with adhesion-related small bowel obstruction[51]

Part 21: Injury to the Urinary Tract during Gynaecological Surgery

Complications include:[52]

Complication	Abdominal	Vaginal	LAVH
Bladder	1%–2%	0.5–1.5%	1%
Ureter	0.1–0.5%	0.05–0.1%	0.19%
Vesicovaginal fistula	0.1–0.2%	0.1–0.2%	0.22%

Table 8: Complications from injury to the urinary tract during gynaecological surgery

10% of ureteral injuries and 33% of bladder injuries are detected at the time of gynaecological surgery without intra-operative cystoscopy.[53]

In developed countries almost 90% of bladder injuries (vesicovaginal fistula) are attributed predominantly to inadvertent bladder injury during pelvic surgery. These injuries include unrecognised intra-operative laceration, bladder wall injury from electrocautery or mechanical crushing, and the dissection of the bladder into an incorrect plane causing a vascular necrosis.

More than 80% of genito-urinary fistulas arise from gynaecological surgery for benign disease (excluding PID, endometriosis and carcinoma).

5% of urogenital fistula cases are associated with obstetrics trauma, including vaginal lacerations from forceps rotation, caesarean delivery, hysterectomy and ruptured uterus. Radiotherapy and surgery for malignant gynaecological disease accounts for a further 5% of fistulae.

Risk factors that pre-dispose to genitourinary fistula
- Prior pelvic surgery
- Vaginal surgery, previous PID
- Ischaemia, diabetes, arteriosclerosis
- Endometriosis
- Distortion by uterine myomas and infection
- Post-operative cuff abscess
- Sub-urethral sling procedures
- Surgical repair of urethral diverticulum
- Electrocautery of bladder papilloma
- Surgery for pelvic carcinomas

Part 21: Injury to the Urinary Tract during Gynaecological Surgery

The incidence of urinary tract injury due to LAVH is 4.9/1000 procedures (3.9/1000 for urinary bladder and 1.0/1000 for ureteral injury).

Prior caesarean section is the most common risk factor for bladder injuries.

75.7% of injuries occur during an operation. 96% of urinary bladder injuries are detected and treated while only 50% of the ureteral are injuries identified during surgery.[54]

Ureteric Injury

Injury to the ureter is one of the most serious complications of gynaecological surgery, and is a common reason for medical litigation. Incidence of ureteric injuries varies from 0.1–1.5%.[55] (42% of ureteral injury is due to urological surgical procedure followed by 34% due to gynaecological procedure.) Gynaecological operations that can lead to it are:
- total abdominal hysterectomy for benign diseases
- vaginal hysterectomy for benign diseases
- total abdominal hysterectomy for gynaecological malignancy
- pelvic clearance for malignancies
- excision of large ovarian tumour (complex adnexectomy)
- intrapartum hysterectomy
- radical hysterectomy
- laparoscopic surgery
- bladder neck suspension and pelvic organ prolapsed.

More than 51% of injuries occur after operations for a benign disease. Therefore, the emphasis should be on reliable procedures for safeguarding the ureter in every gynaecological procedure.

Less than 40% of ureteric damage is recognised intra-operatively. More than 60% of injury is not diagnosed until the post-operative period and most cases present as obstructive symptoms. Hydronephrosis or silent kidney diagnosed by IVU is helpful in diagnosing most cases.

Adequate and timely management (suturing, ligature removal, end-to-end anastomosis, re-implantation of the ureter) is successful in almost all cases. Post-operative management is more difficult. Ureteric catheterisation or surgical re-exploration is necessary in most cases.

Whether an initial conservative approach or immediate operative intervention is the best approach is a controversial subject. However, early surgery, as soon as an accurate diagnosis of the type of damage is made, is the best line of action. Delayed repair is preferable only in higher risk cases and in patients with small fistula.

The long-term outcome after ureteric repair operations is good; almost 100% of patients recover fully with minimum morbidity. Prevention of ureteric injury should be continuously in the minds of gynaecological surgeons during pelvic procedures. Immediate recognition and repair of damage is of paramount importance to avoid prolonged post-operative morbidity and serious long-term ill effects.

Injury of the Rectum during Vaginal Surgery

Injury involves the small intestines in 75% and the large intestines in 25%. 69% of the intestinal injuries are minor.

37.5% of bowel injury occurs during entrance into the peritoneal cavity, 35.2% during separation of adhesions, 10.2% during laparoscopy, 8.6% during vaginal operations, and 8.6% during dilatation and curettage/evacuation.

28% are at risk of a bowel injury as a result of extensive adhesions or involvement of bowel by neoplasms, infections, or endometriosis.

The incidence of rectal injury is 0.7%. Rectal injuries are rare complications of vaginal hysterectomy or transvaginal colpopexy; therefore it's difficult to evaluate their management and outcome.

Rectal laceration is more common when the surgery is done for vaginal vault prolapse with enterocele (in a woman who has undergone a previous vaginal hysterectomy). Rectal injury can also occur where the operation is performed for gender problems.

Rectal laceration usually occurs just above the perineum during the attempt to develop the rectovaginal space. If the injury is recognised early and is repaired promptly it results in good primary healing. The decision on whether to proceed with the operation must depend on the patient's condition and the severity of the problem.[56, 57]

Part 22: Complications of Hysteroscopy

Hysteroscopy is one of the most common investigations carried out for the detection of endometrial pathology. Usually diagnostic hysteroscopy is a simple procedure and has negligible side effects. However, very serious complications can occur in cases where hysteroscopy is used for therapeutic purposes.

Patients who have had previous uterine or cervical surgery are at an increased risk of serious and frequent complications.

Complication rate in diagnostic hysteroscopy (0.012%)[58]
- Perforation
- Haemorrhage
- Bleeding and nonvisualisation of uterine cavity
- Failure of cervical dilatation
- Infection
- Vaginal discharge
- Adhesion
- Pain

Specific for Operative Hysteroscopy

Complications from operative hysteroscopy are much higher, more common and potentially more serious. Most serious complications occur due to operative error.

Complications
- Conversion
- Possibility of hysterectomy
- Technical failure of equipment
- Burn due to heated saline/equipment
- Post-operative infection (uterine/urinary tract)
- Blood transfusion (very rare)
- Cancer after ablation – patients with abnormal bleeding at risk of developing endometrial cancer should be treated with hysterectomy
- Pregnancy after ablation – miscarriage, placenta accreta and preterm labour increased

---

Apart from all common complications occurring due to anaesthetics and positioning of patients, other specific complications of hysteroscopy are the following:

Complications due to the Distension Media[59]

Use of non-electrolytic fluid during electrosurgery avoids the risk of burns to other organs. Other complications are dependent on the type and amount of distension media absorbed. Strict fluid input and output chart should be maintained to avoid fluid overload during hysteroscopic procedure.

1 Use of carbon dioxide during diagnostic hysteroscopy causes cardiac arrhythmia, which can be avoided if correct insufflators are used (rate of less than 100 ml per minute.
2. High molecular weight fluid such as Dextran 70 is seldom used due to anaphylactic reactions (causing adult onset respiratory distress syndrome or ARDS) or pulmonary oedema.
3. Low molecular weight fluid such as saline may be used with a laser.

Saline produces a simple hypervolaemic state, which may be treated by insertion of a central venous line, administration of a diuretic, oxygen and if necessary, cardiac stimulants.

Overload with glycine may produce nausea and vertigo, hyponatraemia, transient hypertension followed by hypotension associated with confusion and disorientation encephalopathy and rarely death. Hyponatremia can be easily treated with administration of diuretics and hypertonic saline solution combined with the monitoring of serum electrolyte.

Complication can be minimised by taking the precautions stated below:

1. Appropriate use of distension media, delivery systems and meticulous accountancy of fluid balance.
2. Keeping operating times to a minimum, fluid pressures below 80 mmHg and gas pressures below 100 mmHg.
3. If the deficit rises to 2 litres or there is evidence of venous congestion, the procedure should be abandoned.

The Surgery

Complications of surgery may arise during the operation such as uterine perforation and haemorrhage. Delayed complications include infection, discharge and adhesion formation.

Uterine Perforation: The incidence of perforation is about 1%.[60] In the British MISTLETOE study, perforation occurred in 0.64% and 0.65% of cases respectively with roller ball and laser.[61] The uterus may be perforated by a dilator, the hysteroscope or by a surgical instrument.

The management will depend:
- on the size, site and whether there is a risk of injury to another organ (e.g. bowel, bladder and vessels).

In addition:

- Simple perforation rarely causes any further damage and may be treated conservatively by observation and appropriate broad spectrum antibiotics.
- Laparoscopy may be considered to exclude bleeding.
- Complex perforation caused by electrosurgical instruments or a laser may be associated with thermal injury to adjacent structures including the bowel or large vessels.
- Lasers may produce thermal injury at a distance from the site of the perforation, because once the myometrium has been breached it will vaporise the next surface in its path.
- If perforation is suspected the energy source should be switched off and hysteroscope left in situ unless laparoscopic monitoring has been in progress, in which case the telescope can be withdrawn.
- If an electrosurgical instrument has caused perforation and concomitant monitoring has been performed, laparoscopic examination to exclude bowel injury may be all that is necessary.
- In cases where a laser is used, laparotomy and detailed examination of the bowel, pelvic blood vessels and aorta is mandatory.

Haemorrhage: The incidence is 2.57% where loop and roller ball have been used. When only one of these has been used the figure is 1.17%.[62]
- Intrauterine bleeding can be controlled by spot electrocoagulation. If this fails then use a tamponade by inserting a Foley catheter and distending balloon.

- The catheter should be left in situ for a few hours.
- If this also fails (deep injury into myometrium/open plexus of vessels) then hysterectomy, ligation or ultrasound-guided embolization of anterior branches of internal iliac arteries may be necessary.
- Tearing of the cervix with tenaculum or uterine perforation may cause less significant bleeding.
- Lateral tears of the cervix may produce significant bleeding and may lead to excessive absorption of the distension medium.

Late onset complications: Infection is rare following hysteroscopic surgery, which can be prevented by prophylactic antibiotics. Treatment should be by appropriate antibiotics following the culture of vaginal swabs and blood.

Vaginal discharge is common after any ablative procedure and is usually self-limiting. Intrauterine adhesions are common, especially after myomectomy. An intrauterine device and administration of oestrogen and progestogen therapy may also help prevent adhesion formation following resection, adhesiolysis or division of the septum.

Failure of resolution of the presenting symptoms: The procedure may fail to cure the presenting symptoms. This may be because of poor patient selection or failure of the surgery.

- Approximately 15% of patients have early pregnancy loss following septum resection. There is also greater risk of third stage complications.
- Myomectomy for menorrhagia or infertility gives disappointing results. About 20% have no immediate improvement and 80% fail to conceive.
- Endometrial ablation produces amenorrhoea in about 30% of cases and satisfactory improvement in about another 50%. 10% will require further surgery in the form of a repeat ablation or hysterectomy.
- Adhesiolysis for Asherman's syndrome is only curative in about 30-40% of cases.

Part 23: Complications of Laparoscopy

	LAVH/TLH (%)	LASH (%)	Total (%)
Minor Complications	1.14	0.99	1.07
Fever >38.5°C (after second day) requiring 5–7 days of antibiotherapy	0.76	0.19	0.47
Bladder incision (<2 cm, sutured by laparoscopy)	0.38	0.25	0.31
Iatrogenic adenomyoma	0.00	0.56	0.28
Major Complications	0.51	0.37	0.44
Haemorrhage	0.06	0.06	0.06
Vesicoperitoneal fistula treated by Foley catheter for 14 days	0.06	0.00	0.03
Ureteral lesions	0.32	0.19	0.25
Rectal perforation	0.06	0.12	0.09
Total Minor and Major Complications	1.59	1.36	1.47

Table 9: Complications in a series of 3190 laparoscopic hysterectomies (1990–2006)[57]

A series of 3190 laparoscopic hysterectomies for benign disease from 1990 to 2006 were evaluated for their complications, comparing vaginal with abdominal procedures.

There have been no national surveys since those carried out by the American Association of Laparoscopists in 1976 and the Royal College of Obstetricians and Gynaecologists in 1977. At that time laparoscopy was virtually confined to diagnostic procedures and sterilisation.

As operative laparoscopy becomes more widely accepted, new techniques are being developed and more surgeons are adopting this form of management. The complication rate can be expected to rise.

The incidence of laparoscopic complications ranges from 1.1% to 5.2% in minor procedures and 2.5% to 6% in major ones.[63] To reduce the prevalence of complications, training programmes must include supervision at all levels of development and there must be a high degree of awareness of potential risks of laparoscopic surgery.

Complications may be associated with:
- the induction of pneumoperitoneum
- insertion of primary and secondary trocar
- the anaesthetic
- thermal instruments
- mechanical instruments
- other associated conditions.

Other associations are:
- The use of steep Trendelenburg positioning and the distension of the abdomen may both reduce excursion of the diaphragm.
- Carbon dioxide (Co2) can be absorbed, particularly during prolonged operations.
- Monitoring by pulse oximetry, the use of endotracheal intubation and positive pressure assisted ventilation reduce the risk of hypercarbia to a minimum.
- If arrhythmia occurs the anaesthetist will be responsible for its management.
- Patients should be returned to the supine position and pneumoperitoneum should be released followed by the discontinuation of surgery. Vasovagal reflex may produce shock and collapse.

Complications due to local anaesthetics during laparoscopy:

- **Anxiety:** can be prevented by administration of diazepam 20 mgs orally 1 hr pre-op.
- **Vasovagal reaction:** causes bradycardia and in severe cases cardiac arrest convulsion and shock. Treatment includes atropine 0.5 mgs IV and oxygen by endotracheal tube at the rate of 4–6 litres/min, adrenaline 0.5–1 ml of 1/100,000 solution slow IV, respiratory and cardiac resuscitation.
- **Pain:** can be prevented by non-steroidal anti-inflammatory drugs (mefenemic acid, naproxen or fentanyl).
- **Conversion to general anaesthetic:** 2% require general anaesthetic.

- **Allergic reaction and anaphylaxis:** characterised by flushing, palpitation, pruritus, agitation, urticaria, bronchospasm. Treatment depends upon severity of the reaction: includes adrenalin 0.5 mg IV or IM, prednisolone 25 mgs IVI and theophylline 250 mgs IVI, IV fluids and oxygen.

Complications from induction of pneumoperitoneum:

- Extraperitoneal gas insufflation – failure to introduce the Veress needle into the peritoneal cavity producing extra peritoneal emphysema in 2% cases.
- Diagnosis is made by palpation of the crepitus caused by CO_2 under the skin.
- The gas is released and the needle should be reintroduced.
- It is necessary to view through the telescope during its insertion through its cannula.
- The typical spider web appearance caused by preperitoneal insufflation is seen.
- The laparoscope should be withdrawn and gas should be expelled. The needle should be reintroduced for insufflation or open laparoscopy should be carried out.

Mediastinal emphysema: Gas may extend into mediastinum, causing cardiac embarrassment. The laparoscopy must be abandoned and gas expelled as much as possible.

Pneumoomentum: The Veress needle in 2% cases penetrates the omentum, and can cause raised insufflation pressure. Unless the omental blood vessels are punctured there are no consequences.

Injury to GI tract: Bowel penetration should be suspected if there is asymmetric abdominal distension, belching, passing of flatus or faecal odour.
- The GIT should be examined thoroughly for perforation. Faecal soiling demands immediate laparotomy and repair of the bowel.
- It is important to ensure that there has not been a through and through injury of a loop of bowel which is adherent to the peritoneum at the site of insertion.
- A simple needle penetration requires no treatment, but the patient should be kept under observation and given broad-spectrum antibiotics.

Bladder injury: Routine catheterisation of the bladder and proper siting of the needle should prevent bladder penetration.

- If pneumaturia is noted then the needle should be partially withdrawn and pneumoperitoneum is continued.
- The treatment of simple punctures is conservative with broad-spectrum antibiotics.

Blood vessel injury: The Veress needle may penetrate any of the major abdominal or pelvic arteries or veins.

- Minor vascular injuries involving omental or mesenteric are difficult to prevent, during insertion of the insufflating needle.
- Injury is suspected if blood returns up the open needle or if free blood is seen in the peritoneal cavity after insertion of the laparoscope.
- If a puncture is suspected then the needle should be left in place.
- Electrocoagulation or laparoscopic suture may control minimal bleeding. Laparotomy is required where superior mesenteric artery or major blood vessels have been damaged.

Gas embolism: Intravascular insufflation of gas may lead to gas embolism or death.

- It should be prevented by routine use of the aspiration test.
- If it happens the patient should be turned to the left lateral position.
- Cardiac puncture may be necessary to release the gas.

Complications from the distension medium (FLUID): Up to 400 ml of gas may be intravasated without producing changes in the ECG.

- Cardiac arrhythmia may be due to the excessive absorption of CO_2.
- It is important to monitor the intra-abdominal pressure throughout the operation and to use an automatic perforator for all the simplest forms of surgery. This will cut out if the intra-abdominal pressure rises.
- Endotracheal intubation and positive pressure respiration will also help to prevent complications from CO_2 insufflation.

Small bowel obstruction following a closed laparoscopic procedure can occur occasionally due to entrapment of the intestines in the trocar incision. Bowel obstruction is more common after an open procedure, perhaps due to the larger incision, the use of sutures, and the exposure of tissues to air embolism.

Summary of Complications[64, 65, 66]
- Minor procedures   1.1–5.2%
- Major procedures   2.5–6%
- Pain   2%
                                             (post-operative
                                             shoulder pain)
- Extraperitoneal gas insufflation   2%
- Blood vessel injury (major vessels)   0.2:1000
- Bladder and ureteric injury   2.8–5.5:1000
- Bleeding at trocar sites
- Inferior epigastric artery damage
- Gas embolism
- Bowel injury   2.8–5.5:1000
- Port site hernia   1.7:1000
- Pulmonary thromboembolism
- Conversion to open laparotomy   8.5–8.9:1000
- Death due to diagnostic laparoscopy   3–8/100,000
- Laparotomy to repair injury   3–9:1000
- Vasovagal reaction – causes bradycardia and in
  severe cases cardiac arrest, convulsions and shock

Major complications per 1000 operative laparoscopies

By instruments
- Veress needle   2.7
- Large trocar   2.4–2.7
- Accessory trocar   2.5–6.0
- Electrocautery   0.5–2.8
- Laser   1.2
- Pneumoperitoneum   7.4
- Laceration of fallopian tubes, mesosalpinx or
  infundibulo-pelvic ligament

By site of injury
- Veress needle   2.6–11.0
- Bowel   0.6–2.0
- Genitourinary   0.6–1.6
- Nerve   6.1
- Uterine perforation   3.7

Other perforations

• Gas embolism due to direct insufflation of blood vessels	
• Death	0.05–0.3
• Hospitalisation	4.2–27.0
• Hospital readmission	3.1–5.0
• Febrile	2.0
• Infection	1.4–6.5
• Transfusion	2.7–3.2

Complications can be minimised by adhering to the proper technique and experience of the surgeon. However, some of the complications (e.g. blind insertion of the cannula) are unavoidable. A good laparoscopic surgeon should be aware of all potential complications and know how to manage them.

To minimise port site hernias, any incision with a trocar more than size 10 mm should be sutured.

Incorrect insertion of the needle can cause emphysema (peritoneal leads to mediastinal emphysema, however, pneumothorax is rare).

Omental emphysema is usually self-limited but makes visualisation of the abdominal organs difficult.

Part 24: Surgical Management of Excessive Menstrual Loss

In England approximately 38,000 hysterectomies and 10,000 endometrial resection and ablations are undertaken for menstrual problems every year, with ablation resulting in lower satisfaction scores than hysterectomy (78–85% and 89–96% respectively).[67]

Endometrial Ablation/Resection

The MISTLETOE study[68] reported the results of a UK (excluding Scotland) audit into the complications associated with first generation devices and found a total complication rate of 4.4%, including two directly related deaths.

Endometrial ablation/resection represents the most closely studied therapy ever to be introduced to gynaecology. A full benefit is usually seen by twelve months. Relative contraindication is premenstrual dysmenorrhoea.

Adverse events occur more often with transcervical resection of the endometrium (TCRE) than endometrial laser ablation (ELA) and the rollerball (which is the least common but safer procedure).

There is no advantage of second generation techniques over the first generation in terms of outcome for heavy menstrual bleeding or patient satisfaction. However, there are reduced complication rates as they can be done under local anaesthesia. Other complications such as fluid overload, uterine perforation, cervical lacerations and haematometra are less likely. However, nausea and vomiting and uterine cramp are more likely.[69]

Short-term complications[70, 71]

- Periprocedural complication rate   8.5/100
- Serious complication   1.25%
- Overall morbidity   5%
- Mortality   0.25/1000 (similar to hysterectomy)
- Uterine perforation (common with TCRE)   10–15/1000
- False passage   1:700 (approx if mistakenly applied)
- Bowel injury   0.7–1/1000
- Emergency hysterectomy   2–6/1000
- Infection   1:100

- Fluid overload – a potentially fatal clinical syndrome characterised by pulmonary oedema, heart failure, confusion, coma, fits and electrolyte disturbance (hyponatraemia and hyperammoniaemia)
- Pregnancy – ongoing contraceptive use is mandatory in sexually active women (accidental pregnancy after ablation/resection is high risk and termination of pregnancy is recommended)
- Mortality   0.27/1000

Long-term complications
- Haematometra
- Haematosalpinx
- Post-ablation sterilisation syndrome   8.4%
- Further surgery   10–26%
(repeat resection/hysterectomy rates vary between studies)

Haematometra can cause cyclical pain due to pockets of endometrium being unable to communicate and drain to the cervical canal or to the fallopian tubes if sterilised. Patients are often amenorrhoeic.

Indication and contraindication for second generation device are outlined below.

Selection criteria:

- family completed
- continue contraception
- failed medical treatment
- normal size uterus
- willing to have hysterectomy if required.

Contraindications:

- severe pelvic pain
- desire to keep fertility
- malignancy or premalignant condition of uterus.

Part 25: Complications of Hysterectomy

Benefits:
- Cervical screening is no longer required.
- Amenorrhoea is guaranteed.
- Relief from dysmenorrhea/gynaecological pelvic pain is assured.
- Relief of certain premenstrual syndrome (PMS) is achieved.
- High satisfaction rates.
- Prophylactic oopherectomy reduces ovarian cancer risk.
- Long-term reduction in prolapse, bowel and bladder symptoms is reported.
- The majority will have an improved or unchanged sex life.

Adverse events:
- A mortality of 0.25/1000 (almost the same as in ablation).
- The main causes of death are pulmonary embolus and heart disease.

Short-term complications of abdominal hysterectomy

• Bowel injury	0.004% (4/10,000)
• Chest infection	
• Pelvic abscess/infection	0.2%
• Pulmonary embolism/venous thrombosis	0.4%
• Wound and vault haematoma	
• Anaemia	
• Blood transfusion	2.3%
• Return to theatre for bleeding/wound dehiscence	0.7%
• Wound dehiscence	
• Post-operative pyrexia	30–47%
• Urinary tract (bladder/ureter) injury	0.7% (0 at subtotal hysterectomy)
• Unilateral ureteric obstruction	
• Vesicovaginal fistula: after TAH	0.5–2% (0.05%)
• Haemorrhage (more in VH than TAH)	5–15 per 100
• Mortality	3.8/1000, (2.5–6.4/1000)
• Recovery 6–8 weeks	
• Fallopian tube prolapse (very rare)	
• Ovarian remnant syndrome	
• Pelvic abscess/infection	0.2%

Frequent risks[71]
- Wound infection
- Bruising
- Increased frequency of micturation
- Delayed wound closure
- Keloid formation
- Early menopause
- Ovarian remnant syndrone

Oophorectomy for unexpected disease found at hysterectomy should not be performed without consent. All women undergoing hysterectomy should be informed that unexpected disease may be found in one or both ovaries, their wishes (to remove this or not) should be documented.

Severe operative complications occur in 3%. The risk decreases with age and increases with greater parity or history of serious illness. Those with symptomatic fibroids (4.4%) experience more complications than women with dysfunctional uterine bleeding (3.6%).

Laparoscopic procedures (6.1%) doubles the risk of operative complications of abdominal hysterectomy (3.6%).

Short-term complications of vaginal hysterectomy[72]
- Post-operative pyrexia   15%
- Bowel injury   6/1000
- Urinary tract injury
  (injury to bladder, occasionally ureter)   0.2%
- Conversion to abdominal hysterectomy
- Haematoma/vault haematoma
- Infection and pelvic abscess   0.3%
- Pulmonary thromboembolism
- Urinary retention and infection
- Wound breakdown
- Haemorrhage (more in VH)   5–15/100
- Mortality   37/100,000
- Vault prolapse
- Excessive bleeding requiring transfusion/return
  to theatre   2%

Long-term complications
- Posterior wall prolapsed and rectocoele – more common (due to reduced support to vagina)
- Incisional hernia
- Bowel symptoms: frequency and urgency due to autonomic denervation
- Premature menopause – premenopause occurs on average 5 years early
- Psychological consequences – some women feel like they are no longer a whole woman, and also report a feeling of loss
- Bladder symptoms – Detrusor instability
- Persistent non-gynaecological pain/new pelvic pain (similar to ablation/resection)   15%

Following a hysterectomy, the menopause occurs on average five years early. Therefore, HRT is recommended up to the average age of menopause (i.e. 51 years).

Bladder mobilisation causes bladder denervation, which may lead to detrusor instability.

Bowel symptoms (frequency and urgency), occur due to autonomic denervation.

Complications associated with any abdominal or pelvic surgery are atelectasis, wound infection, urinary tract infection, thrombophlebitis and pulmonary embolism.

Complications specific to hysterectomy are:
- Wound disruption after abdominal hysterectomy with evisceration of intestines is generally heralded by a profuse serous discharge from the wound infection (peritoneal fluid) 4–8 days post-operatively. The wound should be explored if evisceration is suspected.
- Intra-operative complications such as bleeding from the infundibulopelvic or utero-ovarian pedicle, the uterine vascular pedicle, or the vaginal cuff can occur. Bleeding from the vaginal cuff can be controlled vaginally during vaginal hysterectomy. However, if bleeding is uncontrolled then laparotomy should be considered.
- Sepsis (common) can occur in both procedures (vaginal and abdominal). Symptoms are fever and lower abdominal pain.

Treatment with parenteral antibiotic is often successful. Administration of prophylactic cephalosporin intra-operatively and for 24 hours post-operatively has proven beneficial in controlling infection in vaginal hysterectomies.

- In cases of pelvic abscess or pelvic haematoma, drainage of the infected material through the vaginal cuff might be necessary.

- Injury to the ureter can occur by placing a suture through the ureter, or it may be clamped and cut if the bladder pillars are not sufficiently reflected laterally when clamping the uterine vessels.

- Post-operative fever and flank pain might develop and a uretero-vaginal fistula or urinoma may become apparent 5–21 days after the operation. If urine begins to leak from the vagina post-operatively, a workup, including cystoscopy and intravenous pyelography, is necessary.

- If bladder repair is necessary, an indwelling catheter (suprapubic or transurethral) should be left on free drainage for 3–7 days.

- Sometimes in rectal injury, colostomy may be needed.

	VH (%)	AH (%)
Minor Complications	0.77	0.73
Fever >38.5°C (after second day) requiring 5–7 days of antibiotherapy	0.33	0.00
Bladder incision	0.44	0.73
Major Complications	0.33	0.49
Ureteral lesions	0.33	0.00
Rectal perforation	0.00	0.49
Blood transfusion	2.2	2.6
Bladder injury	0.7	0.4
Reoperation	0.4	0.2
Total Minor and Major Complications	1.10	1.22

Table 10: Comparison of complications in vaginal hysterectomies (VH) and abdominal hysterectomies (AH)[74]

Part 26: Complications of Dilatation and Curettage (D&C)

It is essential to know the position of the uterus by bimanual examination before any procedure is undertaken. Precaution should be taken where the uterus is acutely anteflexed or retroflexed with cervical stenosis, pregnancy, malignancy or post-menopausal atrophic uterus.

A dilator causes less damage than curette. Damage of the lateral wall of the uterus with the curette involving the broad ligament (uterine artery) can lead to severe haemorrhage and haematoma.

If perforation occurs in a pregnant uterus, laparoscopy should be performed. If there is any evidence of bowel injury, laparotomy is mandatory. Perforation of the anterior or posterior wall is usually not a serious accident, therefore (as long as no bowel or large blood vessels are injured) only close observation is required.

Most common surgical complications of D&C[75, 76]
- Overall complication rate   1.7%
- Haemorrhage
- Infection (D&C should not be done in the presence of an infection)
- Perforation of the uterus leading to damage of the bowel, omentum, mesentery, ureter and fallopian tube
- Laceration of the cervix (laceration of cervix should be repaired intra-operatively/at end of operation)
- Febrile morbidity   0.5%
- Uterine perforation   0.63%
- Asherman's syndrome

Part 27: Complications of Operation related to Stress Urinary Incontinence

Surgical treatment is only recommended after the thorough evaluation and determination of the exact cause of the urinary incontinence. The person considering surgery should be aware of the potential risks as well as the expected benefits of the procedure.

The goal of these surgical procedures is to cure the cause of the stress urinary incontinence, either by supporting the bladder and urethra in its proper position (correcting the urethro-vesical angle), so that it can function properly, or by tightening the urethral sphincter.

All surgery that uses general anaesthesia has a small risk of death or complications such as some risk of infection. Factors decreasing the effectiveness of surgical treatment include obesity, low estrogen levels, long-term (chronic) cough, radiation therapy, age, poor nutrition, and strenuous physical activity.

Burch Colposuspension

The evidence available indicates that open retropubic colposuspension is an effective treatment modality for stress urinary incontinence especially in the long-term. Within the first year of treatment, the overall continence rate is approximately 85 to 90%. After five years, around 70% of patients can expect to be dry. The continence rate after Burch colposuspension falls if previous continence surgery has been performed. In one study the continence rate fell from 84% for a primary procedure to 63% for secondary surgery.[77, 78]

Newer minimal access procedures like tension-free vaginal tape look promising in comparison with open colposuspension, but their long-term performance is not known and closer monitoring of the adverse event profile must be done.

Laparoscopic colposuspension should allow speedier recovery but its relative safety and effectiveness is not yet known and it is not recommended as a routine procedure for the treatment of stress incontinence. The procedure should be performed only by an experienced laparoscopic surgeon working in a multidisciplinary team with expertise in the assessment and treatment of incontinence.[79]

Complications[80]
- Haemorrhage from injury to vaginal venous plexus and accessory obturator nerve
- Voiding difficulties   2–27%
- *De novo* detrusor overactivity   8–27%
- Genitourinary prolapse (enterocele, rectocele)   2.5–26.7%
- Ureteric damage
- Infection
- Failure rate   20%*
- Detrusor instability is common after previous continence surgery[79]

Long-term complications noted with colposuspension [81]
- Prolapse (cystocele, rectocele or enterocele)   4%
- Voiding difficulties/chronic retention   6%
- De novo urgency or urge UI   22%
- Dyspareunia   3%
- Recurrent UTI   5%
- Suprapubic pain/pain at site of suture   2%

* Higher failure rate in the presence of low urethral closure pressure

Sling procedure

Suburethral Sling Operations

Traditional slings seem to be as effective as minimally invasive slings, but have higher rates of adverse effects and the long-term adverse event profile is still unclear. Reliable evidence to clarify management options is lacking.

Complications
- Damage to ureters and bladder
- Erosion of bladder and urethra
- Urinary tract infection
- Haematoma causing bleeding and stitch breakdown
- Granulation tissue in suture line

- Voiding difficulties
- Detrusor instability   10–30%
- The synthetic sling material may wear away the
  tissue of the urethra or vagina
- The surgical thread (sutures) used to attach the sling
  may pull out (this is a higher risk for obese people)
- Infection may occur where cuts (incisions) were made
  to do the surgery
- Rejection of the sling material may occur if the sling was
  not made from the person's own tissue
- Sling reaction and removal   24%
- Problems with sexual function after the surgery
- Sinus tract formation
- Occasional minimal leak   14%
- Rare morning stress incontinence   1%
- Suprafascial staph. aureus groin infection

Almost a third of women who have the urethral sling procedure done using animal tissue have complications. When the procedure is carried out using synthetic material, the complication rate is nearly half. However, if complications occur with synthetic slings, they are generally more severe.

Transvaginal Tape (TVT)[80, 81]

This is used to treat women who have stress incontinence caused by weakened urethral sphincter muscles. A sling is formed by taking a piece of the abdominal tissue (fascia) or a piece of synthetic material and using it to suspend the urethral sphincter. Many modifications of the sling procedure have been developed, including recently the transvaginal tape procedure. This type of sling procedure is performed through smaller incisions and can be done as an outpatient surgery. The reported cure rate is 80–90%.

TVT appears to be a safe and effective treatment for obese women with stress incontinence. It has been reported that 89% of obese women who had TVT surgery were cured of stress incontinence, while 11% experienced improvement in their symptoms.[80, 81, 82, 83]

Complications
- Bladder perforations   4%
- Haematoma   1.5%
- Haemorrhage   1.2%
- Urethral perforation   0.5%
- Nerve injury   0.7%

Post-operative complications reported across the case series
- Voiding problems/urinary retention   11%
- *De novo* urgency, urge UI or DO   6%
- UTI   7%
- Healing problems/wound infection
- Tape rejection   0–3%
- Tape trimmed or removed   1.2%
- Tape erosion   1.1%
- Voiding difficulty described as long-term or requiring
  intermittent self-catheterisation (8 studies)   1.8%
- Pain relating to surgery such as inguinal,
  loin, suprapubic   3.4%
- Cystitis   11%
- Asymptomatic POP was reported in 8% of women
  in one of the studies with the longest follow-up[80, 81, 82, 83]
- Recent evidence suggests that TVT is associated
  with higher incidences when compared with TOT
  of bladder perforation (5.4% versus 0.6%)
  and hematoma formation (9.1% versus 1.5%)
- TOT is associated with a higher incidence of
  vaginal wall perforation than TVT (0.0% versus 3.8%)

The risk of bladder puncture (perforation) appears to be higher than from other treatments for stress incontinence. However, this sort of injury is often relatively minor.

Bladder injury during a TVT procedure is a relatively minor complication resulting from bladder perforation by the introducing needle, and can be identified by a cystoscope used during the procedure. Although practices vary considerably, it has been managed by bladder drainage for periods of 12–48 hours and no long-term sequelae have been reported. Bladder injury during colposuspension requires formal closure and drainage for up to 5 days.

Most complications reported across the case series were intra-operative, and thus the results of all case series are considered together rather than by the duration of follow-up.

Transobturator Foramen Procedures for Stress Urinary Incontinence

Transobturator Tape (TOT)[80]

Complications reported across the studies describing the 'outside-in' technique	
• Bladder perforation	0.5%
• *De novo* urgency	4%
• Urethral perforation	1%
• Urinary incontinence	
Voiding difficulty or retention	2.1%
Vaginal erosion	2.5%
Vaginal perforation	0.7
• Dysuria	
• UTI	
• Persistent vaginal discharge	
• Haemorrhage	
• Hematoma	
• Dyspareunia	
• Vaginal tape erosion	14%

This procedure uses the similar tape to tension-free vaginal tape but a different technique is used to insert this. Transvaginal tape is either inserted by the inside-out or outside-in technique, and tape is positioned without any tension beneath the mid-urethra.

Anterior Colporrhaphy/Paravaginal Repair

Anterior colporrhaphy, needle suspensions, paravaginal defect repair and the Marshall-Marchetti-Krantz (MMK) procedure are not recommended for the treatment of stress UI.[80] A characteristic complication of MMK is osteitis pubis, which occurs in 2.5% of patients who undergo this procedure.

The following are not recommended for stress UI:
- routine use of laparoscopic colposuspension
- synthetic slings using materials other than polypropylene that are not of a macroporous (type 1) construction

- anterior colporraphy, needle suspensions, paravaginal defect repair and the MMK procedure
- autologous fat and polytetrafluoroethylene as intramural bulking agents.

As vaginal procedures, an anterior colporrhaphy is often performed in women when the bladder is prolapsing into the vagina (also called a cystocele). An anterior vaginal repair is performed through a vaginal incision, and a paravaginal repair is performed through either a vaginal or an abdominal incision.

In an anterior repair, the pubocervical fascia (the supportive tissue between the vagina and bladder) is folded and stitched together to bring the bladder and urethra into a proper position. In a paravaginal repair, the pubocervical fascia is stitched to the fascia covering the pelvic floor muscles to support the bladder and urethra.

Studies have shown that the cure rate for stress urinary incontinence from these procedures is only about 40–65%. Other surgeries are more effective; these are usually performed to repair a cystocele, but not for stress urinary incontinence. Such procedures are often performed along with another procedure for stress incontinence, for example a retropubic suspension.

Complications
- Damage to bladder and urethra
- Haemorrhage
- Urinary retention
- Post-operative infection
- Urinary tract infection
- Failure of the procedure
- Recurrence
- Dyspareunia due to vaginal narrowing
- Urinary incontinence in patients with no previous problems

The cure rate is 74%. Incontinence occurs in 10–20% of patients following surgery. This is often an improvement over incontinence present before the surgery. However, in a small number of patients, incontinence can get worse.

Long-term complications reported with needle suspension procedures[83]

• Suprapubic pain/pain at site of suture	6%
• Surgery to release or remove sutures	3%
• *De novo* urgency or urge UI	13%
• Recurrent UTI	2%
• Voiding difficulty	6%
• Dyspareunia	9%
• POP (cystocele, rectocele or enterocele)	2%
• ISC due to retention	2%

Artificial Urinary Sphincter

The use of an artificial urinary sphincter should be considered for the management of stress UI in women only if previous surgery has failed. Lifelong follow-up is recommended.

Artificial urinary sphincters are rarely used in women. Most experts advise their patients to try other treatments first before resorting to this treatment. Artificial sphincters are used only in people with a complete loss of sphincter or urethral control. Installation of an artificial sphincter may be done for:
- reflex incontinence
- severe continual leakage of urine from the urethra
- severe urinary incontinence where other methods of treatment have failed.

Possible complications of the surgery
- Wound infection
- Urethral erosion
- The need for removal of the device
- Failure of the implant to function properly
- Erosion of tissue in the area of the sphincter placement
- The need to possibly modify some activities such as bicycle riding (as the pump mechanism is placed in the labia of the patient)

Collagen Injection[80]

The periurethral (intramural) injection of collagen is a minor surgical procedure. This may be recommended for the treatment of male and female stress incontinence caused by urethral sphincter dysfunction.

This procedure is performed in an outpatient setting with a local or spinal anaesthesia. The procedure may need to be repeated after a few months to achieve bladder control. The collagen injection helps control the urine leakage by bulking up the area around the urethra, thus compressing the sphincter.

Women who were treated with collagen injection therapy reported a higher success rate (75% improved or cured). However, some studies report only a 30%–55% cure rate.

Possible complications that can occur after a collagen injection
- Infection
- Local fibrosis (less dense to diffuse)
- Allergic reaction
- Urine retention
- Potentially serious allergic reaction to collagen
- Reduced physical activity may be required for several days following the procedure
- Repeat injections
- Pain at the injection site

Noticeable improvements may take more than one session of injections.

Any potential candidate for collagen injections must have a skin test prior to treatment to check for an allergic reaction. Materials used for urethral bulking include:
- polytetrafluoroethylene (PTFE)
- bovine collagen (glutaraldehyde cross-linked bovine collagen)
- durasphere.

Collagen used for bulking is obtained from cows and is used after being chemically modified. It may cause allergic reactions in some people. Collagen is absorbed slowly by the body, which makes it necessary to repeat the injections after several years. Collagen therapy is expensive.

Two materials under study for bulking use are silicone and fat taken from the person receiving the urethral bulking. The use of fat as a bulking material eliminates the possibility of allergic reactions. Intramural bulking agents (glutaraldehyde cross-linked collagen, silicone, carbon-coated zirconium beads or hyaluronic acid/dextran copolymer) should be considered for the management of stress UI if conservative management has failed. Women should be made aware that:

- repeat injections may be required to achieve efficacy
- efficacy diminishes with time
- efficacy is inferior to that of retropubic suspension or sling.

Surgery for Overactive Bladder

Sacral Nerve Stimulation[84]

Complications	
• Infection	
• Pain (in abdominal, leg, pelvis and gluteal incision)	11%
• Repositioning	
• Removal of implant	7%
• Surgical revision	
• Technical device problem – loss of effectiveness, battery end of life	11%
• Seroma formation	
• Disturbed bowel function	
• Toe flexion	8%

Botulinum Toxin A

A bladder wall injection with botulinum toxin A (BoNT-A) should be used in the treatment of idiopathic detrusor overactivity only in women who have not responded to conservative treatments, and who are willing and able to self-catheterise. Women should be informed about the lack of long-term data. There should be special arrangements for audit or research. The use of botulinum toxin A for this indication is outside the UK marketing authorisation for the product. Informed consent to treatment should be obtained and documented.[80]

Complications
- Failure of treatment
- Urinary retention
- Incomplete voiding, abdominal pressure to assist voiding
- Haematuria
- Transient dysuria
- Transient retention
- Difficulty urinating
- Feeling of incomplete emptying

Little is known about the effects of repeated injections. With repeated use of BoNT-A, there might be some risk of inducing immunisation against the toxin, with a consequent loss of effect.[85]

Complications of continent urinary diversion
- Death <1%
- Stomal problems e.g. parastomal hernia and upper urinary tract dilatation
- Catheterisation difficulties
- Prolapse of the continent nipple
- Pouch stone formation
- Urinary leakage from pouch
- Metabolic complications
- Excess mucus production
- Urinary infection
- Pouch rupture
- Reflex
- Upper tract deterioration
- Vesicovaginal fistula
- Surgical revision of loop

Complications of Ileocystoplasty (augmentation cystoplasty)

Augmentation cystoplasty for the management of idiopathic detrusor overactivity should be restricted to women who have not responded to conservative treatments and who are willing and able to self-catheterise. Preoperative counselling should include common and serious complications: bowel disturbance, metabolic acidosis, mucus production and/or retention in the bladder, UTI and urinary retention. The small risk of malignancy occurring in the augmented bladder should also be discussed. Lifelong follow-up is recommended.[80]

Early
- Post-operative bleeding   1.5%
- Ileus   1.9%
- Wound infection   1.9%
- Bowel obstruction   3.7%
- Leak from suture line
- Abdominal wall disruption
- Thromboembolism   1%
- Small intestine obstruction   2%

Late
- Mucus in urine   100
- Recurrent urinary tract infection   34%
- Malabsorption or acidosis non-clinical
- Risk of neoplasia unknown
- Retention requiring long-term CISC   40–100
- Cystoplasty rupture   0.9%
- Nocturia
- Lymph collection
- Chronic diarrhoea   12%
- Partial bowel obstruction   8%
- Incisional hernia
- Bladder calculus
- Voiding dysfunction
- Urinary incontinence
- Disturbed bowel habit
  - Increased bowel frequency   22%
  - Fecal incontinence   17%
  - Diarrhoea   11%
  - Constipation   4%
- Mucus plug retention
- Anastomotic leak   2%
- Persistent urinary leak   3%
- Incisional hernia   4–6%
- Calculus formation   2%
- Urethral stricture
- Stone   13%
- Metabolic disturbance   16%

Part 28: Complications of Vaginal Repair

Posterior Colporrhaphy

Posterior colporrhaphy is repair of the posterior vaginal wall. Perineorrhaphy refers to repair of the perineal body. Where posterior colporrhaphy is performed at the same time, the term 'posterior perineorrhaphy' is used.

Complications of perineorrhaphy
- Damage to rectum
- Uncontrolled haemorrhage
- Difficulty in defecation
- Urinary tract infection
- Dyspareunia
- Recurrence of prolapse

Additional risks include the facts that:
- constipation is very common, although most patients have constipation before the surgery
- recurrence of prolapse occurs in 5–10% of abdominal repairs and about 15–25% of perineal repairs.

Manchester Repair

This is a rarely performed operation. It involves amputation of the cervix where conservation of the uterus is desired. This can be performed in cases of mid uterine descent and elongated cervix.

Complications of Manchester Repair
- Infertility
- Increased risk of miscarriage
- Preterm labour
- Dystocia
- High risk of recurrence of prolapse   16%
- High incidence of rectocoele and enterocoele

Sacrospinal Fixation

Post hysterectomy, vault prolapse requires a technique to suspend the apex of the vagina. By this method the sacrospinous ligament is used to suspend the vagina into the hollow of the sacrum.

Complications
- Sacral nerve damage
- Pudendal nerve and vessel injury
- Pain in the buttock and thigh/pins and needle
- Pulmonary thromboembolism
- Haemorrhage – primary and secondary
- Haematoma
- Infection
- Urinary tract infection
- Injury to rectum and bladder and ureter
- Constipation
- Worsening bladder symptoms (urge/stress incontinence)
- Recurrent vaginal prolapse   2.4%
- Shortened vaginal syndrome

Part 29: Complications and Counselling for Female Sterilisation

- To avoid medico-legal problems, consent should not be taken during stress or in an emergency situation.
- Full gynaecological history and a pelvic examination should be carried out to exclude pathology such as endometriosis or fibroids where a more radical procedure might be indicated.
- A detailed menstrual history should be taken to exclude pregnancy (confirm with pregnancy test).

Women seeking a sterilisation must be counselled effectively about a number of important issues such as:

- Vasectomy as an alternative for married or cohabiting women. Vasectomy is technically easier and safer. Failure is 1:2000 and the chance of a reversal is high.
- Potential for failure and possibility of ectopic pregnancy (1–3 per 1000 procedures).
- Potential irreversibility of female sterilisation. Women should be told that the procedure will be permanent.
- Description of the procedure, possible complications such as damage to the small or large bowel, gas embolism, injury to blood vessels, including the aorta and internal iliac artery (such complications are very uncommon).
- Preoperative contraception advice – women using an oral contraceptive should be advised to continue the pill to the time of the procedure and until completion of their cycle.
- Luteal phase pregnancy cannot be avoided unless all sterilisation takes place during the menstrual or follicular phase.
- IUCD users should be advised to abstain from intercourse in the cycle before admission for surgery.
- D&C is not recommended unless as a clinical indication for endometrial biopsy.
- Post-operative menstrual changes after tubal occlusion have no valid scientific evidence of an increased incidence of menorrhagia.
- An information leaflet should be given to the patient before the operation.

Complications of laparoscopic sterilisation[86]

• Death	1 in 12,000
• Conversion to laparotomy	1–2%
• Failure rate	1 in 200
• Ectopic pregnancy	0.03–0.27%
• Permanent regret	6% (>20% for 30 years or younger)
• Bowel perforation	3 in 1000

Reasons for regret:

- Being sterilised at a young age (<25 years).
- Operation done at an apparently convenient time (after caesarean section or immediately after a difficult labour or delivery).
- A relationship crisis at the time of sterilisation and a subsequent new partner. Women who were well informed and had enough time and opportunity to make up their mind were less likely to ask for a reversal.

Part 30: Complications
of Termination of Pregnancy

Complications may be immediate (within 3 hours of the operation), intermediate (3 hours to 28 days) and late (thereafter). Haemorrhage has been reported from 0.5% to 4.5%. The rate of transfusion is 0.6% to 0.32%.

Failed Abortion (continued intrauterine or ectopic pregnancy)

Failure to terminate the pregnancy is relatively common with very early abortions (<6 wk GA). Such patients may present to the emergency department with symptoms of continuing pregnancy such as hyperemesis, increased abdominal girth, and breast engorgement. In addition, an unrecognised ectopic pregnancy in the post-abortion period presents in the usual manner.[87]

Mortality	1 in 100,000 (in first trimester)	
Infection rate	<1% in elective	
Uterine perforation	0.5%	
	<13 weeks	>13 weeks
Sepsis	0.2%	0.2%
Haemorrhage	0.9%	3.2%
Perforation	1.8 (1/250)	4.3 (0.32%)
Retained product	0.5%	0.2%
Failure	2–4% (medical) 1% (surgical)	
Endometritis/PID	1%	
Incomplete	5–10%	
Delayed bleeding	Rate increasing	
Asherman's syndrome		
Delayed sequelae	Post-traumatic stress	
Adenomyosis	Increasing high rate	
Placenta praevia	Increased risk	
Cervical trauma	1%	
Post-abortion infection	10%	

Table 11: Complications of abortion

Risk factors for perforation:
- Previous termination of pregnancy.
- Lower segment caesarean section.
- Loop excision of cervix (scarring of the internal os).

Part 31: Complications of ERPC (Evacuation of Retained Product of Conception)

Complications of spontaneous miscarriage and therapeutic abortion include complications of anaesthesia, hematometra, retained products of conception, uterine perforation, bowel and bladder injury, failure of procedure, septic miscarriage, cervical shock, cervical laceration, post-abortion triad (i.e. pain, bleeding, low-grade fever), and disseminated intravascular coagulation (DIC).

Post-abortion complications develop as a result of three major mechanisms, incomplete evacuation of the uterus and uterine atony, which leads to hemorrhagic complications, infection, and instrumental injury.

Frequency depends on gestational age (GA) at the time of abortion and method of abortion. Complication rates according to GA at the time of abortion are:
1. fewer than 8 weeks, less than 1%
2. 8–12 weeks, 1.5–2%
3. 12–13 weeks, 3–6%
4. second trimester, up to 50%, possibly higher.

Mortality and morbidity depend on GA at the time of abortion. Mortality rates per 100,000 abortions are:
1. fewer than 8 weeks, 0.5%
2. 11–12 weeks, 2.2%
3. 16–20 weeks, 14%
4. more than 21 weeks, 18%.

Although intra-operative and early post-operative complications are rarely seen, these include those outlined below.

Complications
• Due to local anaesthesia
• Due to general anaesthesia
• Cervical shock
• Post-abortion triad
• Haemorrhage
• Haematometra
• Perforation
• Bowel injury
• Bladder injury
• Septic abortion
• DIC

Paracervical block is the most common method of anaesthesia for a therapeutic abortion. Intravascular injection is a potentially life-threatening complication of this method that can lead to convulsion, cardiopulmonary arrest, and death.

Complications with general anaesthesia may lead to uterine atony with severe haemorrhage.

Vasovagal syncope produced by stimulation of the cervical canal during dilatation may occur. Rapid recovery usually follows.

Pain, bleeding, and low-grade fevers are the most common presenting complaints (post-abortion triad), usually caused by retained products of conception.

Excessive haemorrhage, during or after abortion, may signify uterine atony, cervical laceration, uterine perforation, cervical pregnancy, a more advanced gestation than anticipated, or coagulopathy.

Patients with uterine perforation missed during the procedure usually present with increased abdominal pain, bleeding (possibly ranging from very mild to absent), and fever. If perforation results in injury to major blood vessels, patients may present in haemorrhagic shock.

Bowel injury may accompany uterine perforation. If initially unrecognised, patients present with abdominal pain, fever, blood in the stool, nausea, and vomiting.

Bladder injury occurs as a result of uterine or cervical perforation. Patients present with suprapubic pain and haematuria. Patients present with fever, chills, abdominal pain, and vaginal bleeding.

DIC should be suspected in patients who present with severe post-abortion bleeding (especially after mid-trimester abortions). Incidence is approximately 200 cases per 100,000 abortions; this rate is even higher for saline instillation techniques (660 per 100,000 abortions).

Part 32: Complications of Colposcopy and Cervical Biopsy

A colposcopy is used to look at the vagina, vulva, and cervix, and it is also used to take cervical biopsy. This test may be done after having abnormal Pap test results indicating an infection, a pre-cancerous growth, or cancer. It is also used to get a closer look at areas of the vagina, cervix, and vulva that do not appear normal.

Ideally, it should not be done during a menstrual period, and the woman should avoid douching or sexual intercourse within 24 hours of the test.

Some women describe a pinching sensation during the procedure. Others experience menstrual-like cramping for a short time afterwards.

There may be slight spotting or bleeding for a few days after the biopsy. The woman may have a little dark-coloured, sandy discharge from the vagina for a few days after the procedure and the feeling of a little light-headedness right after the test.

Complications
- Infection
- Pain: after the biopsy may experience some pain, similar to menstrual cramping
- Light bleeding: may have some bleeding or other vaginal discharge, but these will gradually disappear

---

Thick black discharge after a biopsy can occur which may be caused by an AgNo3 or Monsel's solution that is placed on the area to help stop bleeding. This discharge may last for a few days.

To reduce the chance of infection, sexual intercourse should be avoided (48 to 72 hours after the procedure). Tampons should not be used for two weeks, and vaginal douches should be avoided for a while.

Cone Biopsy
This procedure is used to see if the cancer cells have spread to tissue beneath the surface of the cervix. It is also used to treat very early and very small tumours. A cone biopsy takes a cone-shaped piece of tissue from a deeper part of the cervix. It is usually done with a scalpel, laser or electrosurgical loop.

Side effects
- Infection
- Light bleeding or cramping
- Effects on conception

Most side effects are temporary and go away in time. Cramp and light bleeding (discharge) are common for a few days. Sometimes a small cotton vaginal pack is necessary to help stop the bleeding. Women should be advised to avoid doing anything too physically strenuous for about three weeks as this could make some bleed more heavily. If the bleeding lasts longer than two weeks or becomes heavy, women should be reviewed in case of secondary infection.

To prevent infection, sexual intercourse and tampons should be avoided for two to three weeks. This also gives time for the cervix to heal.[88]

Effects on conception include:
- The cervix incompetence: prophylactic cervical suture early in the pregnancy can reduce the chance of this happening.
- Cervical dystocia due to scarring: causes failure to progress in labour and increases the chance of caesarean section.
- Fertility: it seems reasonable to conclude that the operation has no extraordinary effect on the ability to become pregnant and to deliver.
- Perforation: the perforations do not create any serious problems, either immediate or delayed.
- Delayed bleeding.

Large Loop Excision of the Transformation Zone
Another method that removes a small sample of the cervix for examination under a microscope is called a large loop excision of the transformation zone (LLETZ). A loop of wire carrying an electric current is used to gently scoop the cells from the surface of the cervix. This procedure takes about 10 minutes and may be done under local anaesthetic in the doctor's office or in hospital under general anaesthetic.

Side effects
- Infection
- Vaginal bleeding or cramping

Complications of LLETZ/Cone Biopsy

This is indicated for both diagnostic and therapeutic cases. The most common side effects of cone biopsy include cramping/discomfort and moderate or mild bleeding for a few weeks after the procedure. Patients should avoid sexual intercourse, tampons and douching until the incision is completely healed, which may take several weeks. Patients should also discuss other possible side effects of cone biopsy prior to the procedure, especially after large loop excision either done by large loop or traditional knife cone biopsy.

Complications	
• Haemorrhage (primary and secondary)	87%
• Infection (local or leading to PID)	
• Thromboembolism	
• Post-operative pain	67%
• Haematometra	
• Uterine perforation	
• Cervical stenosis and distortion	
• Cervical incompetence	
• Discharge	63%
• Change to first period colposcopy	71%

Bleeding is the most common complication within the first 24 hours. Cone biopsy is notorious for secondary haemorrhage, which usually happens after 10 days. Pelvic infection secondary to cervical cone biopsy can result in pain, bleeding and discharge.

There are no long-term studies that have specifically evaluated small loop excisions with respect to fertility and childbirth. However, the effect (damage) on the cervix is identical to, and, in most cases, less than that associated with other procedures such as cryotherapy (freezing therapy), laser therapy, electrocautery or surgical conization. With the exception of deep cervical conization, none of these procedures have been associated with infertility, pregnancy loss, or premature labour.[89]

Results from the TOMBOLA trial have shown that unless a loop excision is unusually extensive, it is likely there will be no increased risk of side effects.[90]

Part 33: Marsupialization of a Bartholin's Cyst

Scarring and stenosis of the duct leads to the formation of a chronic mucoid-filled cysts.

Complications
Complications
• Recurrence
• Dyspareunia
• Chronic pain
• Bleeding
• Haematoma formation

Recurrence is very common and usually associated with incomplete removal of the cyst or abscess rather than marsupialization. The marsupialized opening should be kept wide. The incision should be made on the fold of labia majora and minora to avoid dyspareunia at a later stage.

Part 34: Vaginal Pessaries

Although vaginal pessaries have been used for a long time they are usually used as a temporary measure for (initial management) the treatment of utero-vaginal prolapse. They are also used in patients who do not desire surgery or are not fit for surgery. Follow-ups are individualised but adequate follow-up is essential to minimise minor and major complications associated with vaginal pessaries.

Rare Complications
- Herniation and incarceration of the cervix and even the small bowel
- Unilateral/bilateral hydronephrosis with urosepsis and even uraemia
- Chronic irritation with prolonged continuous use can cause vaginal cancer (new pessaries are made up of inert material)
- Pessary incarceration within the vagina with formation of vaginal adhesions
- Fistulae
- Complete erosion with transmigration of the pessary into the bladder or the rectum
- Recurrence

Pessaries remain helpful for patients with genital prolapse who refuse or are not able to have surgery due to medical complications. It is generally considered both conservative and safe to wear a vaginal pessary. Only a few cases of severe complications have been reported, most resulting from a neglected pessary.[91, 92]

Common Complications of Vaginal Pessaries	**%**
• Bleeding	46.8
• Extrusion	27.6
• Vaginal discharge	25.5
• Pain/constipation	25.5
• Incontinence	3.19
• Theatre for removal	1.19

- 40.4% experienced more than one type of complication
- 31.1% experienced more than one episode
- 17.2% experienced more than two episodes
- 12.9% experienced more than three episodes
- 21.5% experienced more than four episodes[93]

Part 35: Complications of Radical Vulvar Surgery and Groin Lymphadenectomy[94]

Early (up to six weeks)
- Anaesthesia of anterior thigh (secondary after surgery) to femoral nerve injury
- Deep venous thrombosis
- Groin wound infection
- Wound breakdown   30–50%
- Skin necrosis
- Haemorrhage
- Osteitis pubis
- Pulmonary embolism
- Seroma of the femoral triangle   10–20%
- Urinary tract infection
- Wound necrosis

Late (six weeks and after)
- Chronic leg edema (surgery or later)   10%
- Dyspareunia
- Femoral hernia
- Genital prolapse
- Recurrent leg lymphangitis
- Urinary stress incontinence
- Psychological problems due to altered body image
- Impaired sexual function
- Hernia formation (due to division of inguinal ligament)
- Spraying of urinary stream

Part 36: Complications of Artificial Reproductive Techniques

Complications of In Vitro Fertilisation[95–101]

Complications
- Cancellation of treatment due to failure to respond to the drug stimulation
- Side effects of drugs
- Vaginal bleeding following the egg collection
- Technical difficulty at the time of embryo transfer
- Ovarian hyperstimulation syndrome
  - Mild   33%
  - Moderate to severe   3–8%
- Multiple pregnancy
- Ectopic pregnancy
- Prematurity
- Congenital malformation
- Very low birth weight
- IUGR
- Stillbirth   Increased 4 times
- Neonatal death
- Miscarriage

Complications of IVF/ICSI (Intracytoplasmic Sperm Inoculation)

Complications
- Damage to egg during piercing   15% eggs lost this way
- Increased risk of carrying karyotype anomaly
- Sex chromosomal anomalies if immature spermatids used for ICSI
- Male children may have decreased fertility themselves
- Ectopic pregnancy   2–5%
- Congenital and/or genetic abnormality   3.3% (major anomaly, same as general population)

Risk of genital and breast cancer: The effects of ovulation induction agents currently used in ART on genital and breast cancer risks are unclear. Further follow-up is required in this area.[101]

Risk of congenital anomalies and malignancy in newborns: Two meta-analyses comparing birth defects in IVF and ICSI infants with spontaneously conceived controls showed a statistically significant increased risk of birth defects in infants conceived after IVF or ICSI of the order of 30–40%.[102, 103]

Risk of malignancy in children: An increased risk of retinoblastoma and langerhans histiocytosis has been reported. Larger studies are required for reliable evaluation of any increase in risk amongst ART children.[104]

Complications of Intrauterine Insemination

Complications
• Failure
• Ovarian hyperstimulation
• Multiple pregnancy
• Enlargement of ovaries
• Pain and discomfort in abdomen
• Infection

Risks of Donor Insemination

For the most part the risks of donor insemination are no different from those of becoming pregnant naturally, but the following points must be considered.

Side effects of clomiphene used for ovulation induction
• Nausea
• Vomiting
• Breast tenderness
• Bloatedness
• Ovarian cyst
• Dizziness
• Grand mal epilepsy
• Hallucination

Complications
• Infection
• Fetal abnormality
• Miscarriage
• Consanguinity
• Failure to conceive
• Legal situation

Donors should be screened for hepatitis and HIV, as in theory any infection that could be transmitted sexually could also be transmitted by donor insemination.

There is always a small risk of fetal anomaly. However, a risk is reduced with donor insemination. Donors are screened to avoid any that have personal or family history of fetal anomaly.

As almost 20% of pregnancies miscarry in the general population, the risk remains the same with donor insemination.

Failure to conceive is the most common problem that could be considered a risk of donor insemination.

A child from donor insemination now has the same legal status as the natural child of a married couple. When the couple are not married but jointly agree to donor insemination treatment, the child will be the legal child of both partners. There is no legal requirement to tell a child born from donor insemination about their origin but there are strong arguments for doing so. As everybody has a right to know about his or her origins such information should be available on question.

**Complications of ovulation induction
(hyperstimulation syndrome)**
- Pain
- Weight gain
- Ovarian enlargement
- Torsion of ovaries
- Increased capillary permeability leading to:
  - Oedema
  - Ascitis
  - Pleural effusion
  - Pericardial effusion
- Haemoconcentration
- Blood clotting disorder leading to:
  - Stroke
  - Pulmonary embolism
- Liver dysfunction (hepatocellular and cholestatic changes)
- Renal impairment (prerenal failure)
- Acute respiratory distress syndrome

- • Obstetrics complications:
    Increased incidence of early pregnancy loss
    Low birth weight
    Preterm labour
    Hypertension
    Abruption

Part 37: Contraception

Failure rate of contraception[105, 106, 107]

• Dutch cap	2.3 per 100 women/years (%)
• Male sterilisation	0.05
• Female sterilisation	0.5
• COC	0.2–0.3
• POP	0.3–5
• IUCD copper	0.3–4
• Mirena	0.09
• Condom	2–15
• Diaphragm & spermicide	5
• Etonogestrel implant	0–0.07
• Depo-Provera	<0.5
• Coitus interruptus	30
• Rhythm method	30–40
• None	60–70

Complications of Contraceptive Usage

Combined Contraceptive Pill

Venous thromboembolism (VTE) is a rare complication associated with COCs. However, the level of risk is dependent on the type of progestogens contained. The risk of VTE in the case of Yasmin (contains drosiprenone instead of progestogen) is comparable to other COCs.

COCs should be prescribed with caution to women who are obese (BMI >30) and who have a higher baseline risk of VTE.[108, 109]

Complications
- Venous thrombemolism
- Arterial disease
- Small rise in blood sugar
- Liver disease
- Small increased risk of breast cancer
- Bloating
- Weight gain due to water retention

- Breast tenderness
- Nausea
- Chloasma
- Headache
- Non-infective vaginal discharge
- Acne
- Greasy hair
- Hirsutism
- Depression

Progesterone-only Pill

These are less effective than combined pills, 2–6 per 100 women/years.

Complications
- Alteration of menstrual pattern (irregular low grade breakthrough bleeding)
- Functional ovarian cysts in 50% of pill users
- Ectopic pregnancy (if failure)
- Efficacy depends on compliance
- Skin rash
- Breast fullness
- Depression
- Breast cancer increase

Injectables and Implants

Complications
- Severe disturbance of menstruation
- Can take up to 9 months to wear off its effect
- Amenorrhea
- Weight gain   60%
- Mood swings
- Depression
- Decrease bone density
- Persistent infertility up to 22 months
- Bloating
- Breast tenderness
- Injection cannot be removed once given
- Minor surgical procedure required for removal and insertion of implant

IUCD[108, 109]

Complications

• Perforation	1.2 per 1000
• Expulsion	2.5–12.5 per 100 (over 2–12 years)

- Infection
- Long heavy periods (less with Mirena)
- Dysmenorrhea
- Failure
- Risk of miscarriage (if failure occurs)
- Ectopic pregnancy (if failure occurs, less with Mirena)
- Functional ovarian cyst (Mirena coil)
- Irregular bleeding during initial period (Mirena coil)
- No protection against STDs
- Menorrhagia
- Intermenstrual bleeding
- Allergic reaction due to copper content

Perforation is rare but common during postpartum, after termination or during breast feeding. Infection is more likely in the 3 weeks after fitting. Ideally, HVS and chlamydial swabs should be taken before fitting.

Copper IUCDs do not increase the overall risk of ectopic pregnancy but do increase the relative risk ectopic pregnancy.

Emergency Contraception

The overall risk of pregnancy after a single act of unprotected intercourse on any day in the cycle is between 2–4%. However, this is highest during the time of ovulation (20–30%).

It is not guaranteed that at the time of menstruation pregnancy will not occur, therefore emergency contraception (ECP) should be given to all women (no contraindication) requesting within 72 hours of intercourse.

Levonelle is a progestogen-only ECP that is licensed to prevent pregnancy when taken within 72 hours of unprotected intercourse. ECPs do not prevent 100% of pregnancies and are more effective the sooner they are taken after unprotected intercourse. Levonelle has been shown to be safer and more effective than the previously used Yuzpe method (oestrogen and progestogen).

Time Taken after Intercourse	Proportion of Pregnancies Prevented
24 hours or less	95%
25–48 hours	85%
49–72 hours	58%

Table 11: Efficacy of Levonelle (levonorgestrel 0.75 mg)

- Women should be encouraged to seek treatment as early as possible after unprotected sex and advised that treatment failure may occur.
- Women who do not have a normal period after using Levonelle should be followed up so that pregnancy can be excluded.
- The possibility of ectopic pregnancy should be considered, particularly in women with a previous ectopic pregnancy, tubal surgery or pelvic inflammatory disease.

IUCD had 99.9% efficacy and can be given up to five days after intercourse.

Side effects associated with the use of ECPs usually taper off within a day or two.

Complications
- Nausea
- Vomiting
- Headache
- Dizziness
- Diarrhoea
- Failure
- Other complications of progestogens
- Complications of IUCD (perforation, infection, discomfort and pain)
- Breast tenderness
- Irregular bleeding

Half of the women who take the combined pills feel nauseous, but only for about 24 hours. Less than one out of five women vomit with combined pills. The risk of nausea and vomiting is lower with progestin-only ECPs.

Frequent use of ECPs may cause periods to become irregular and unpredictable. The side effects of anti-nausea medication may include drowsiness. Please follow the precautions on the package insert.

Ulipristal acetate (ellaOne®) is a selective progesterone receptor modulator licensed for emergency contraception up to 120 hours after unprotected sexual intercourse (UPSI) or contraceptive failure. The primary mechanism is inhibition or delay of ovulation. Alterations to the endometrium may also contribute to efficacy. It is effective up to 120 hours after unprotected sexual intercourse. Side effects are similar to other progesterone-only emergency contraception. No serious reactions have been reported so far.[108, 110]

Part 38: Hormone Replacement Therapy[111–121]

Review of the Evidence on Long-Term Safety of HRT

The recent publication of a major US study, Women's Health Initiative (WHI) oestrogen-only HRT, WHI Memory Study (WHIMS), MWS (Million Women Study), HABITS trial has been examined and current evidence of long-term safety of HRT reviewed.[111, 112]

HRT advice for prescribers based on these studies is outlined below.

- For the treatment of menopausal symptoms the benefits of short-term HRT are considered to outweigh the risks in the majority of cases.
- The decision to start HRT should be made on an individual basis with full information given to the woman.
- The lowest effective dose for the shortest possible time should be given and the need should be reviewed annually.
- HRT should be used for the prevention of osteoporosis in women over 50 years and there is an increased risk of fracture only where other osteoporosis therapy is contraindicated or in those who are intolerant to this therapy.
- Healthy women who have no menopausal symptoms should be advised against HRT as the risks outweigh the benefits.
- HRT does not prevent coronary heart disease or a decline in cognitive function, and should not be prescribed for this purpose.
- HRT is contraindicated in women with breast cancer.
- Oestrogen-only therapy is appropriate in hysterectomised women.
- Combined HRT is indicated in non-hysterectomised women. Women should be fully counselled regarding the added risk of breast cancer and should fully participate in decision making.
- Women taking HRT to relieve menopausal symptoms will benefit from the effect of HRT on osteoporosis.

Complications of HRT

For the majority of women with menopausal symptoms that affect their quality of life, the risk is generally small and is outweighed by the benefits of short-term treatment. Counselling regarding benefits and risks should be discussed.

Breast Cancer

The MWS[112] did demonstrate an association between HRT and an increased risk of invasive cancer that increases with duration of use. Combined estrogen and progestin use for more than five years doubles the risk each year.

The risk increases within a few years of use and falls after stopping to the same level within five years as women not taking HRT. The relative risk is significantly greater for combined HRT than oestrogen-only, irrespective of the type of progestogens and its sequential or continuous addition to oestrogen.

New data from the MWS confirms that HRT adversely affects the sensitivity and specificity of mammography, and therefore also the radiological detection of breast cancer.[113]

Specificity may last for up to five years after stopping HRT. Consequently, stopping HRT a few weeks before a mammography is of no benefit.

The HABITS trial suggests that HRT may increase the recurrence of breast cancer in women who had previously had the disease. Therefore, HRT is contraindicated in women who have previously had breast cancer. The recent decline in breast cancer is related to the decreased use of HRT.

Coronary Heart Disease (CHD)

WHI and HERS (Heart and Oestrogen Replacement Study) both have shown possible increases in the risk of coronary heart disease in the first year, and no evidence of overall benefits up to five years' use.[114, 115] Oestrogen-only HRT also did not show any cardio protection.

New analysis of two hormone trials from the WHI demonstrated that the risk of heart attack is not increased in menopausal women who started HRT less than ten years after menopause. The risk increases if it is started ten years after menopause. Hormone therapy should not be used for the prevention of heart attacks. If hormones do not increase risk of heart attack at younger ages – and even if they reduce risk in these age groups – there is no certainty that any benefit will persist with long-term use into older ages.[116, 117]

- HRT in women aged 50–59 years does not increase CHD risk in healthy women, and may even decrease the risk in this age group.
- Oestrogen-alone therapy in the age group 50–59 was associated with significantly less coronary calcification (equivalent to a smaller plaque burden), which is consistent with findings of a lower coronary intervention score in women of this age in the WHI study.
- Early harm (more coronary events during the first two years of HRT) was not observed in the early post-menopausal period. The number of CHD events decreased with duration of HRT in both WHI clinical trials.
- Data derived from randomized controlled trials in the age group 50–59 are similar to the older observational data suggesting a protective effect of HRT on coronary disease.

Stroke
The WHI trial has suggested an increased risk of stroke in HRT users for both combined and oestrogen-only. Oestrogen plus progestin increases the risk of ischemic stroke in generally healthy postmenopausal women. The risk of stroke from hormones does not depend on when a woman starts hormone therapy; strokes are increased regardless of years since menopause.[118]

Cognitive Function
A WHIMS study has suggested HRT use after the age of 65 years, (conjugated equine oestrogen) did not protect against cognitive impairment or probable dementia.

Combined oestrogen and MPA doubles the risk of probable dementia significantly in women over the age of 75. Based on the available evidence, ERT or HRT cannot be recommended for overall cognitive improvement or maintenance in older postmenopausal women without cognitive impairment.[119]

VTE
HRT has shown to have an increased risk of DVT and PE in the vast majority of studies, being greatest in the first year of use.

Endometrial CA
Endometrial hyperplasia and cancer increases with increasing dose and duration with the use of unopposed oestrogen. However, the addition of progestogen for at least 12 days per month greatly reduces the risk.

Ovarian Cancer

There is a small increase in the risk of ovarian cancer in hysterectomised women after long-term oestrogen-only HRT. Women who use HRT are at an increased risk of both incident and fatal ovarian cancer.[120]

Use of HRT after Hysterectomy for Endometriosis

Women taking HRT immediately after total abdominal hysterectomy and bilateral salpingo-oophorectomy are at no greater risk of recurrent pain than those who delay HRT for more than six weeks.

Women who had TAH with conservation of ovaries are at a six times greater risk of developing recurrent pain and eight times risk of re-operation.

The surgically castrated woman in early age should not be confused with a postmenopausal older woman with hot flushes. In the young woman whose ovaries have been removed surgically and who has no contraindications to oestrogen (e.g. breast cancer or other hormone-sensitive tumour), oestrogen therapy is appropriate and should be considered true replacement therapy. Without oestrogen therapy, young surgically castrated women are likely to experience debilitating vasomotor symptoms and sexual dysfunction as a result of genital atrophy. This also leads to accelerated loss of bone density, which can cause osteopenia or osteoporosis. Oestrogen therapy should be continued until the patient is of normal menopausal age (early to mid 50s). Following this it will depend on whether symptoms are present after ceasing therapy.

Higher than usual doses of oestrogen are often appropriate (the 35 year old with surgical menopause may need 1.25 mg of conjugated equine oestrogen, 2 mg of estradiol, or a 0.1 mg estradiol patch) for adequate symptom relief. In comparison, 0.625 mg of conjugated equine estrogen, 1 mg of estradiol, or a 0.05 mg estradiol patch often represents appropriate doses for the older menopausal woman with hot flushes.

In women who experience spontaneous menopause in their 50s, use of hormone therapy is discretionary for the treatment of menopausal symptoms.

Part 39: Potential Complications of Vaginoplasty

Vaginoplasty involves the creation or reshaping of the vagina. The procedure is sometimes performed to revise vaginal anomalies or congenital conditions such as the absence of a vagina at birth, as well as to repair the area following disease or injury.[121]

As with other procedures like plastic surgery of the nose (rhinoplasty), vaginoplasty may be undertaken for functional reasons, aesthetic reasons, or a combination of the two.

Vaginoplasty evokes very strong emotional responses (both pro and con) far more often than more common procedures like rhinoplasty. There is considerable controversy regarding surgery on some patients, notably children with 'ambiguous genitalia' who have no pressing medical or functional need.

Vaginoplasty is currently required by law in order for women in our community to change the designation of their sex on many government documents. Therefore, it is considered in the eyes of the law to be medically necessary for full social and legal recognition as females. It also has the added therapeutic benefits of bringing minds and bodies into congruence.

Most serious complications
- **Death:** some of the complications below are potentially fatal
- **Fistula:** between the colon and the vagina
- **Blood loss:** massive haemorrhage requiring many units of blood (up to 15 units) can occur
- **Thromboembolism**
- **Infection**
- **Pneumonia**
- **Necrosis**
- **Vaginal collapse** (in severe cases of stenosis the entire new vagina can cave in, which may lead to reconstruction and in severe case its removal)
- **Paralysis:** caused by stroke from a blood clot, or a severed nerve (extremely rare)
- **Allergic reaction**

Complications related to the bowel and bladder
- **Bowel problems:** permanent problems in case of development of fistula during vaginoplasty involving a bowel segment (sigmoid vaginoplasty)
- **Urinary problems:** permanent urinary problems, due to change in stream direction, incontinence or painful urination. Urethra can be very wide causing problems, or it may stick out or have remnant spongy penile tissue around it, which can cause irritation when sitting or walking.
- **Sexual function:** lack of orgasm
- **Stenosis:** vagina too narrow
- **Depth problems:** vagina too shallow
- **Lubrication**
- **Numbness**
- **Pain**
- **Hypersensitivity:** some areas too sensitive to be touched (can also cause discomfort just from walking or sitting)
- **Cosmetic**
- **Scarring:** some people have noticeable scarring that is discoloured or raised
- **Graft:** some patients require a skin graft, which can mean additional scars
- **Keloids:** some (notably African-American patients) get this unusual type of raised red scars
- **Hair:** some patients have reported hair growth inside the vagina and around the opening, this is difficult to remove after vaginoplasty, and is the reason many advise getting electrolysis prior to vaginoplasty
- **Clitoris size:** some women have a clitoris that is much larger than typical, others have one that is small
- **Shape:** asymmetrical outcomes are not uncommon, especially in one-stage procedures
- **Labia:** sometimes labia are different shapes or positioned differently
- **Urethra:** some have a urine stream that points in an unusual direction, others have had a urethra opening that is big enough for a partner to mistake for the vaginal opening
- **Positioning:** some have reported the entire vulva is too high or too low, or that there is too much or too little space between the clitoris and the vaginal opening
- **Yeast infection/douching:** some have temporary, and in some cases, chronic problems with yeast infections or an unpleasant smell following surgery

Psychological complications
- **Fatigue:** many find that they tire easily in the months following surgery
- **Depression:** many find that completion of vaginoplasty leaves them feeling a bit lost, especially if they had expectations that vaginoplasty would make a major difference to their day-to-day existence
- **Regret (did not put in proper thought):** in rare cases, patients have decided that vaginoplasty was not the solution to their unhappiness, others have had vaginoplasty because all they wanted was the surgery, and had no success in living as females

Temporary complications
- **Evacuation:** many have problems going to the bathroom for a while after surgery, from constipation and haemorrhoids, to an inability to control the bladder, sometimes requiring incontinence pads, which usually resolves itself in a few months
- **Mild bleeding:** many have mild bleeding, especially around sutures or after dilation, which requires the use of a sanitary pad for a few months
- **Bed sores:** those who do not move around enough sometimes get bed sores, which can take a while to heal
- **Ripped suture:** occasionally someone might tear a suture from certain types of movement, and while usually not a serious problem, it can cause a small scar
- **Clitoral scab:** many report they have a scab over their clitoris following surgery and in some cases when this falls off there is very little protruding clitoral tissue remaining, which can be corrected during labiaplasty if desired
- **Shocks:** many report a sensation of electrical 'shocks' as nerves in the surgical site regenerate, which is especially common in the legs near the pelvis
- **Bruising:** ranging from mild to significant, which can take many weeks to resolve
- **Nausea:** following anaesthesia, antibiotics
- **Allergic reaction (drugs, leg things, etc.):** some patients get contact dermatitis from leg compression stockings, the catheter, or from other vaginoplasty related items

Problems with Lubrication

Some people achieve moderate amounts of prostatic lubrication, but must usually supplement it. Conversely, those who have sigmoid vaginoplasty sometimes secrete so much mucus from the bowel segment in their vagina that they must wear maxi pads at all times.

References

1. Sheehan HL & Murdoch R. Postpartum necrosis of the anterior pituitary. *Journal of Obstetrics and Gynaecology of the British Empire.* 1938, (45): 456–89.
2. Snooks SJ et al. Risk factors in childbirth causing damage to the pelvic floor innervations. *British Journal of Surgery.* 1985, (72) Suppl. S15–S17.
3. Abraham S et al. Recovery after childbirth: a preliminary prospective study. *Medical Journal of Australia.* 1990, 152(1): 9–12.
4. Sultan AH & Thakar R. Lower genital tract and anal sphincter trauma. *Best Practice and Research in Clinical Obstetrics and Gynaecology.* 2002, 16(1): 99–115.
5. Mann T. *Clinical guidelines to improve patient care within the NHS.* London: NHS Executive. 1996.
6. O'Grady JP. *Vacuum Extraction Introduction and History.* 2002. e-medicine.   http://www.emedicine.com/med/topic3389.htm (accessed 16/9/11).
7. Cunningham G et al. *Williams Obstetrics* (21st edn). USA: McGraw Hill. 2001.
8. Johanson R & Menon V. Soft versus rigid vacuum extractor cups for assisted vaginal delivery. *Cochrane Database of Systematic Reviews.* 2000, Issue 2.
9. Johanson RB et al. A randomised prospective study comparing the new vacuum extractor policy with forceps delivery. *British Journal of Obstetrics and Gynaecology.* 1993, 100(6): 524–30.
10. Wen SW et al. Comparison of maternal and infant outcomes between vacuum extraction and forceps deliveries. *American Journal of Epidemiology.* 2001, 153(2): 103–7.
11. Towner D et al. Effect of mode of delivery in nulliparous women on neonatal intracranial injury. *New England Journal of Medicine.* 1999, 341(23): 1709–14.
12. RCOG. *Operative Vaginal Delivery.* Consent Advice No 11.
13. RCOG. *Caesarean Section.* Consent Advice No 7.

14. Bergholt T et al. Intraoperative surgical complication during caesarean section: an observational study of the incidence and risk factors. *Acta Obstet. Gynaecol. Scand.* 2003, 82(3): 251–6.

15. Lumbiganon P et al. Method of delivery and pregnancy outcomes in Asia: The WHO global survey on maternal and perinatal health 2007–2008. *Lancet.* 2010, 375(9713): 490–9.

16. Smail F & Hofmeyr GJ. Antibiotic prophylaxis for caesarean section. *Cochrane Database Systematic Review.* 2002, Issue 3, CD000933.

17. James AH et al. Venous thromboembolism during pregnancy and the postpartum period: incidence, risk factors and mortality. *Am. J. Obstet. Gynecol.* 2007, 196(2) e24.

18. Silver RM et al. Maternal morbidity associated with multiple repeat cesarean deliveries. *Obstet. Gynecol.* 2006, 107(6): 1226–32.

19. Milosević J et al. Placental complication after a previous caesarean section. *Med Pregl.* 2009, 62(5–6): 212–6.

20. Brumfield CG et al. Puerperal infection after caesarean delivery: evaluation of a standardized protocol. *Am. J. Obstet. Gynecol.* 2000, 182(5): 1147–51.

21. Ravasia DJ, Wood SL & Pollard JK. Uterine rupture during induced trial of labour among women with previous caesarean delivery. *Am. J. Obstet. Gynecol.* 2000, 183(5): 1176–9.

22. Zelop CM et al. Uterine rupture during induced trials of labour in women with a previous caesarean delivery. *Am. J. Obstet. Gynecol.* 1999, 181(4): 882–6.

23. Simonazzi G et al. Amniocentesis and chorionic villus sampling in twin gestations: which is the best sampling technique? *Am. J. Obstet. Gynecol.* 2010, 202(4): 365 e1–5.

24. Papp C & Papp Z. Chorionic villus sampling and amniocentesis: what are the risks in current practice? *Current Opinion in Obstetrics and Gynaecology.* 2003, 15(2): 159–65.

25. Stetten G et al. Reevaluating confined placental mosaicism. *Am. J. Med. Genet. A.* 2004, 131(3): 232–9.

26. Drakeley AL, Roberts D & Alfirevic Z. Cervical cerclage for prevention of preterm delivery: meta-analysis of randomized trials. *Obstetrics and Gynaecology.* 2003, 102(3): 621–7.

27. Ventur, SJ et al. Births: final data for 1997. *National Vital Statistics Reports.* 1999, 47(18): 1–96.

28. Lau TK et al. Pregnancy outcome after successful external cephalic version at term. *American Journal of Obstetrics and Gynaecology.* 1997 176(1 Pt 1): 218–23.

29. RCOG. *Guideline External Cephalic Version and Reducing the Incidence of Breech Presentation.* (Green-Top 22a).

30. Smith KC & Starke J. Bacille Calmette-Guérin vaccine. In: SA Plotkins, WA Orenstein & PA Offit (eds) *Vaccines.* (4th edn). Philadelphia: WB Saunders. 2003.

31. Magann EF et al. Maternal morbidity and mortality associated with intrauterine fetal demise. *Southern Medical Journal.* 2001, 95(5): 493–5.

32. Reid DE et al. Maternal afibrinogenemia associated with long-standing intrauterine fetal death. *American Journal of Obstetrics and Gynaecology.* 1953, 66(3): 500–6.

33. Confidential Enquiry into Maternal and Child Health (CEMACH): *Perinatal Mortality 2007.* 2009. United Kingdom.

34. Rådestad I et al. Psychological complications after stillbirth – influence of memories and immediate management: population based study. *BMJ.* 1996, 312(7045): 1505–8.

35. Wagaarachchi PT et al. Medical management of late intrauterine death using a combination of mifepristone and misoprostol. *British Journal of Obstetrics and Gynaecology.* 2002, 109(4): 443–7.

36. Bernstein PS. Shoulder dystocia – reducing the legal risk. *Obstetrics and Gynaecology and Women's Health.* 2004, 9(2). http://www.medscape.com/viewarticle/490554 (accessed 16/9/11).

37. Aroma U & Lahdensuu M et al. Severe complications associated with epidural and spinal anaesthesia in Finland 1987–1993. A study based on patient insurance claims. *Acta Anaesthesia Scandinavica.* 1997, 41(4): 445–52.

38. Casey WF. Spinal Anaesthesia – a Practical Guide. *Update in Anaesthesia.* 2002, (12). http://web.squ.edu.om/med-Lib/MED_CD/E_CDs/health%20development/html/clients/WAWF SA/html/u12/u1208_01.htm (accessed 16/9/11).

39. Fink BR. History of Neural Blockade. In: MJ Cousins & PO Bridenbaugh (eds) *Neural Blockade in Clinical Anesthesia and Management of Pain.* (2nd edn). Philadelphia: Lippincott Williams and Wilkins. 1988.

40. Cope RW. The Woolley and Roe case. *Anaesthesia.* 1995, 50(2): 162–75.

41. Chadwick HS et al. A comparison of obstetric and nonobstetric anesthesia malpractice claims. *Anesthesiology.* 1991, 74(2): 242–9.

42. Breen TW et al. Factors associated with back pain after childbirth. *Anesthesiology.* 1994, 81(1): 29–34.

43. Macdonald R. A dural puncture rate of 1% is unacceptable in epidural practice. *International Journal of Obstetric Anaesthesia.* *1994,* 3(1): 50–1.
44. Brownridge P. The management of headache following accidental dural puncture in obstetric patients. *Anaesth. Intensive Care.* 1983, 11(1): 4–15.
45. Ong GY et al. Paresthesias and motor dysfunction after labour and delivery. *Anaesthesia and Analgesia.* 1987, 66(1): 18–22.
46. Scottish Intercollegiate Guidelines Network 2002. *Prophylaxis of Venous Thromboembolism.* Edinburgh: SIGN.
47. Cardosi RJ, Cox CS & Hoffman MS. Post-operative neuropathies after major pelvic surgery. *Obstetrics and Gynaecology.* 2002, 100(2): 240–4.
48. Rhodes JC et al. Hysterectomy and sexual functioning. *JAMA.* 1999, 282(20): 1934–41.
49. Halmesmäki K et al. The effect of hysterectomy or levonorgestrel-releasing intrauterine system on sexual functioning among women with menorrhagia: a 5-year randomised controlled trial. *BJOG.* 2007, 114(5): 563–8.
50. Mokate T, Wright C & Mander T. Hysterectomy and sexual function. *J Br Menopause* Soc. 2006, 12(4): 153–7.
51. Al-Took S, Platt R & Tulandi T. Adhesion-related small-bowel obstruction after gynaecologic operations. *American Journal of Obstetrics and Gynaecology.* 1999, 180 (2 Pt 1): 313–5.
52. Rock JA. *TeLinde's Operative Gynaecology.* Philadelphia: Lippincott Williams and Wilkins. (10th edn). 2011.
53. Dwyer PL. Urinary tract injury: medical negligence or unavoidable complication? *Int Urogynecol J Pelvic Floor Dysfunct.* 2010, 21(8): 903–10.
54. Soong YK et al. Urinary tract injury in laparoscopic-assisted vaginal hysterectomy. *J Minim Invasive Gyecol. 2007,* 14(5): 600–5.
55. Sakellariou P et al. Management of ureteric injuries during gynaecological operations: 10 year's experience. *Euro J Obstet Gynaecol Reprod Biol.* 2002, 101(2): 179–84.
56. Hoffman MS et al. Injury of the rectum during vaginal surgery. *Am J Obstet Gynaecol.* 1999, 181(2): 274–7.
57. Gordon, AG. *Complications of hysteroscopy.* E-Lecture. http://www.gfmer.ch/Books/Endoscopy_book/Ch23_Complications_Lap.html (accessed 16/9/11).
58. Krebs HB. Intestinal injury in gynaecologic surgery: a ten-year experience. *Am J Obstet Gynecol.* 1986, 155(3): 509–14.

59. Siegler AM. *Therapeutic Hysteroscopy: Indications and Techniques.* USA: Mosby. 1990.
60. Lewis BV. Guidelines for endometrial ablation. *BJOG.* 1994, 101(6): 470–3.
61. Maresh MM & Khaled KM. Audit in obstetrics. *Current Opinion in Obstetrics and Gynaecology.* 1996, 8(4): 296–9.
62. Donnez O et al. A series of 3190 laparoscopic hysterectomies for benign disease from 1990 to 2006: evaluation of complications compared with vaginal and abdominal procedures. *BJOG.* 2009, 116(4): 492–500.
63. Kane MG & Krejs GJ. Complications of diagnostic laparoscopy in Dallas: a 7-year prospective study. *Gastrointestinal Endoscopy.* 1984, 30(40): 237–40.
64. Asch R. & Studd JWW. *Progress in Reproductive Endocrinology.* Edinburgh: Churchill Livingtone. 1996.
65. Levy BS & Hulka JF et al. Complications associated with laparoscopy. *J Am Assoc Gynaecol Laparosc.* 1994, 1(4 pt 1): 301–5.
66. RCOG. *Consent for Laparoscopy.* Consent Advice no. 2. (2nd edn.) 2008.
67. Department of Health. *Hospital Episodes Statistic.* http://www.dh.gov.uk/en/Publicationsandstatistics/Statistics/HospitalEpisodeStatistics/index.htm (accessed 16/9/11).
68. Overton C, Hargreaves J & Maresh M. A national survey of the complications of endometrial destruction for menstrual disorders: the MISTLETOE study. Minimally invasive surgical techniques – Laser, EndoThermal or Endoresection. *Br J Obstet Gynaecol.* 1997, 104(12): 1351–9.
69. Lethaby, A et al. Endometrial resection/ablation techniques for heavy menstrual bleeding. *Cochrane Database Syst Rev.* 2009, 7(4) CD 001501.
70. Spies JB et al. Complications after uterine artery embolization for leiomyomas. *Obstetrics & Gynaecology.* 2002, 100(5 Pt 1): 873–80.
71. RCOG. *Abdominal Hysterectomy for Benign Conditions.* Consent Advice No 4. http://www.rcog.org.uk/files/rcog-corp/CA4-15072010.pdf (accessed 16/9/11). London: RCOG. 2009.
72. RCOG. *Obtaining Valid Consent.* Clinical Governance Advice No 6. London: RCOG. http://www.rcog.org.uk/files/rcog-corp/CGA6-15072010.pdf (accessed 16/9/11). London: RCOG. 2008.
73. McPherson, K et al. Severe complications of hysterectomy: the VALUE study. *BJOG.* 2004, 111(7): 688–94.

74. Doğanay M & et al. Abdominal vaginal and total laparoscopic hysterectomy: perioperative morbidity. *Arch Gynaecol Obstet.* 2010 Sep 16.

75. MacKenzie IZ & Bibby JG. Critical assessment of dilatation and curettage in 1029 women. *Lancet.* 1978, 2(8089): 566–8.

76. McElin TW et al. Diagnostic dilatation and curettage. A 20-year survey. *Obstetrics and Gynaecology.* 1969, 33(6): 807–12.

77. Alcalay M, Monga A & Stanton S. Burch colposuspension: a 10–20 year follow up. *Br J Obstet Gynaecol.* 1995, 102(9): 740–5.

78. Galloway NT, Davies N & Stephenson TP. The complications of colposuspension. *Br J Urol* 1987, 60(2): 122–4.

79. Lapitan MC, Cody JD & Grant A. Open retropubic colposuspension for urinary incontinence in women. *Cochrane Database Syst Rev.* 2009, 7(4) CD002912.

80. NICE. *Urinary incontinence CG40.* http://www.nice.org.uk/CG40 (accessed 16/9/11). 2009.

81. Pushkar DY et al. Complications of mid-urethral slings for treatment of stress urinary incontinence. *Int J Gynaecol Obstet.* 2011, 113(1): 54–7.

82. Nichols FH & Delancey JOL. Clinical Problems, *Injuries and Complications of Gynaecologic Surgery.* (3rd edn). Baltimore: Williams & Wilkins. 1988.

83. Rehman H et al. Traditional suburethral sling operations for urinary incontinence in women. *Cochrane Database Syst Rev.* 2011, 19(1) CD001754.

84. Pettit P. Current opinion: complications and troubleshooting of sacral neuromodulation. *Int Urogynaecol J Pelvic Floor Dysfunct.* 2010, Dec; 21 Suppl 2: S491–6.

85. Schmid DM et al. Prospects and limitations of treatment with botulinum neurotoxin type A for patients with refractory idiopathic detrusor overactivity. *BJU Int.* 2008 Jul 25; 102 Suppl 1:7–10.

86. RCOG. *Laparoscopic Tubal Occlusion.* Consent Advice 3. http://www.rcog.org.uk/files/rcog-corp/uploaded-files/*Consent3Laparoscopictubal2004*.pdf (accessed 16/9/11). 2004.

87. Trupin SR. *Elective Abortion.*http://emedicine.medscape.com/article/252560-overview (accessed 16/9/11).

88. Schulman H & Ferguson JH. Cone biopsy of the cervix. A review of 486 cases. *J Obstet Gynaecol Br Emp.* 1962 Jun; 69: 474–80.

89. Kyrgiou M et al. Obstetric outcomes after conservative treatment for intraepithelial or early invasive cervical lesions: systematic review and meta-analysis. *Lancet.* 2006, 367(9509): 489–98.

90. TOMBOLA (Trial of Management of Borderline and Other Low-

grade Abnormal Smears) Group. After-effects reported by women following colposcopy, cervical biopsies and LLETZ: results from the TOMBOLA trial. *BJOG.* 2009, 116(11): 1506–14.

91. Alnaif B & Drutz HP. Bacterial vaginosis increases in pessary users. *International Urogynaecology Journal & Pelvic Floor Dysfunction.* 2000, 11(4): 219–22.

92. Bash KL. Review of vaginal pessaries. *Obstetric and Gynaecological Survey.* 2000, 55(7): 455–60.

93. Sarma S, Ying T & Mooore KH. Long-term vaginal ring pessary use: discontinuation rates and adverse events. *BJOG.* 2009, 116(13): 1715–21.

94. Rock JA. Vulvar Surgery. In: *TeLinde's Operative Gynecology.* (10th edn). Philadelphia: Lippincott Williams and Wilkins. 2011.

95. Clayton HB et al. Ectopic pregnancy risk with assisted reproductive technology procedures. *Obstet Gynecol.* 2006, 107(3): 595–604.

96. Wisborg K, Ingerslev HJ, Henriksen TB. IVF and stillbirth: a prospective follow-up study. *Hum Reprod.* 2010, 25(5): 1312–6.

97. Allen C et al. Pregnancy and perinatal outcomes after assisted reproduction: a comparative study. *Ir J Med Sci.* 2008, 177(3): 233–41.

98. Mathur R, Kailasam C & Jenkins J. Review of the evidence base of strategies to prevent ovarian hyperstimulation syndrome. *Hum Fertil (Camb).* 2007, 10(2): 75–8.

99. http://www.hfea.gov.uk (accessed 16/9/11).

100. McDonald SD et al. Perinatal outcomes of singleton pregnancies achieved by in vitro fertilization: a systematic review and meta-analysis. *J Obstet Gynaecol Can.* 2005, 27(5): 449–59.

101. Shaw RW. *Gynaecology.* (4th edn). Edinburgh: Churchill Livingstone. 2010.

102. Hansen M et al. Assisted reproductive technologies and the risk of birth defects – a systematic review. *Hum Reprod.* 2005 Feb, 20(2): 328–38.

103. Rimm AA et al. A meta-analysis of controlled studies comparing major malformation rates in IVF and ICSI infants with naturally conceived children. *J Assist Reprod Genet.* 2004, 21(12): 437–43.

104. Bradbury BD & Jick H. In vitro fertilization and childhood retinoblastoma. *Br J Clin Pharmacol.* 2004, 58(2): 209–11.

105. Long-acting progestogen-only contraception. *Drug and Therapeutics Bulletin.* 1996, 34(12): 93–6.

106. BNF 7:3

107. NICE. *Long-acting reversible contraception.* October 2005. RCOG Press: London. http://www.nice.org.uk/CG030 (accessed 16/9/11).
108. Faculty of Family Planning and Reproductive Health Care. http://www.ffprhc.org.uk/ (accessed 16/9/11).
109. World Health Organisation. *Medical Eigibility Criteria for Contraceptive Use.* (4th edn). 2010. http://whqlibdoc.who.int/publications/2010/9789241563888_eng.pdf (accessed 16/9/11).
110. Randomised controlled trial of levonorgestrel versus the Yuzpe regimen of combined oral contraceptives for emergency contraception. Task force on Postovulatory Methods of Fertility Regulation. *Lancet.* 1998, 352(9126): 428–33.
111. Holmberg L et al. HABITS (hormonal replacement therapy after breast cancer – is it safe?), a randomised comparison: trial stopped. *Lancet.* 2004, 363(9407): 453–7.
112. Rossouw JE et al. Postmenopausal hormone therapy and risk of cardiovascular disease by age and years since menopause. *JAMA.* 2007, 297(13): 1465–77.
113. Chlebowski RT et al. Estrogen plus progestin and breast cancer detection by means of mammography and breast biopsy. *Arch Intern Med.* 2008, 168(4): 370–7.
114. Manson JE et al. Estrogen therapy and coronary-artery calcification. *N Eng J Med.* 2007, 356(25): 2591–602.
115. Lobo RA. Evaluation of cardiovascular event rates with hormone therapy in healthy, early postmenopausal women: results from 2 large clinical trials. *Arch Intern Med.* 2004, 164(5): 482–4.
116. Grodstein F, Manson JE & Stampfer MJ. Hormone therapy and coronary heart disease: the role of time since menopause and age at hormone initiation. *J Women's Health.* 2006, 15(1): 35–44.
117. Lethaby A et al. Hormone replacement therapy for cognitive function in postmenopausal women. *Cochrane Database of Syst Rev.* 2008, Jan 23;(1) CD003122.
118. Beral V et al. Ovarian cancer and hormone replacement therapy in the Million Women Study. *Lancet.* 2007, 369(9574): 1703–10.
119. Hendrix SL et al. Effects of conjugated equine estrogen on stroke in the Women's Health Initiative. *Circulation.* 2006, 113(20): 2425–34.
120. Shlipak MG et al. Lipid changes on hormone therapy and coronary heart disease events in the Heart and Estrogen/progestin Replacement Study (HERS). *American Heart Journal.* 2003, 146(5): 870–5.

121. Transsexual   Road   Map.   *Vaginoplasty.*
http://www.tsroadmap.com/physical/vaginoplasty   (accessed
16/9/11).

Appendix 1: Common General Post-Operative Complications

First day pyrexia is usually low grade and is due to a metabolic response to trauma to the tissues and an inflammatory response (release of cytokines).

Some drugs, IV fluid, blood or blood products may cause pyrexia due to release of pyrogens. Sometimes local IV lines can cause a local inflammatory reaction.

Lung infection or UTI is more apparent if the urinary catheter is left for a long period. Prophylactic antibiotics should be used to avoid this.

After these infections, complication is associated with deep-seated abscesses.

With the use of prophylactic antibiotics wound infection has reduced from 20–30 to less than 10%.

Causes of Post-Operative Pyrexia
Day 1–3: (early)
- Local and systemic drug reaction
- Secondary lung complication (atelectasis)
- Response to tissue trauma
- Pyrogens due to IV fluids, blood transfusion
- Urinary tract infection due to catheterisation

Day 4–6: (intermediate)
- Chest infection
- Wound infection
- UTI
- Infection to IV cannula site
- DVT

Day 7–10: (late)
- Wound abscess
- Chest infection
- UTI due to prolonged catheterisation
- DVT, Pulmonary embolism
- Pelvic abscess

Appendix 2: Complications of Common Procedures in Obstetrics and Gynaecology

Abdominal sacral colpopexy: Bleeding, infection, trauma to pelvic organs including bowel, bladder, ureters, nerves, vessels, incontinence, recurrence of prolapse

Anterior colporrhaphy: Bleeding, infection, trauma to bladder, urinary incontinence, inability to urinate requiring catheterisation or further surgery

Bartholin's cyst excision: Bleeding, return of abscess or cyst, need for further surgery

Burch colposuspension: Bleeding, infection, trauma to pelvic organs including bowel, bladder, ureters, nerves, vessels, recurrence of incontinence, may require short-term self catheterisation

Caesarean section: Bleeding, infection, trauma to pelvic organs (including bowel, bladder, ureters, nerves, vessels), trauma to baby, further surgery (including hysterectomy and/or oophorectomy)

Cerclage: Bleeding, infection, rupture of membranes, injury to cervix, failure

Colpocleisis: Bleeding, infection, trauma to pelvic organs including bowel, bladder, ureters, nerves, vessels, incontinence, recurrence of prolapse, inability to have vaginal intercourse

Cone biopsy: Bleeding, infection, cervical incompetence, cervical stenosis, need for further surgery

Diagnostic laparoscopy: Bleeding, infection, trauma to pelvic organs including bowel, bladder, ureters, nerves, vessels, need for laparotomy

Dilatation and curettage: Bleeding, perforation resulting in infection, trauma to pelvic organs (including bowel, bladder, ureters, nerves, vessels), Asherman's syndrome, need for diagnostic laparoscopy if lateral perforation, need for additional surgery including hysterectomy if life-threatening bleeding, retained abnormal tissue requiring further surgery

Endometrial ablation: Bleeding, infection, perforation of uterus, fluid overload, need for hysterectomy, damage to bowel, continued bleeding

Enterocoele repair: Bleeding, infection, trauma to rectum and bowel, recurrence, dyspareunia

Forceps or vacuum extraction: Injury to birth canal tissues, trauma to baby, failure requiring caesarean section

Hysteroscopy: Bleeding, infection, perforation of uterus, fluid overload

IUD Insertion: Bleeding, infection, perforation of uterus, infertility

Laser ablation of vulvar lesions: Bleeding, infection, pain, tissue burns, returns of VIN requiring further surgery

LSTL: Bleeding, infection, trauma to pelvic organs including bowel, bladder, nerves, vessels, ureters, need for laparotomy, failure

Myomectomy: Bleeding, infection, trauma to pelvic organs including bowel, bladder, ureters, nerves, vessels, return of fibroids, need for hysterectomy

Oocyte retrieval: Bleeding, infection, trauma to bowel, ovaries, inability to retrieve eggs

Oophorectomy: Bleeding, infection, trauma to pelvic organs including bowel, bladder, ureters, nerves, vessels, ovarian remnant syndrome, possible staging laparotomy

Placental removal: Bleeding, infection, perforation resulting in trauma to pelvic organs (including bowel, bladder, ureters, nerves, and vessels), need for hysterectomy

Posterior colporrhaphy: Bleeding, infection, trauma to rectum and bowel, recurrence, dyspareunia

Pubovaginal sling: Bleeding, infection, trauma to pelvic organs including bowel, bladder, ureters, nerves, vessels, recurrent incontinence, 1–2% long-term voiding dysfunction requiring catheterisation

Reconstructive tubal surgery: Bleeding, infection, infertility (failure)

Rectovaginal fistulas: Bleeding, infection, trauma to pelvic organs including rectum and bowel, failure of procedure

Sacrospinous ligament suspension: Bleeding, infection, trauma to pelvic organs including bowel, bladder, ureters, nerves, vessels, incontinence, recurrence of prolapse

Salpingectomy: Bleeding, infection, trauma to pelvic organs including bowel, bladder, ureters, nerves, vessels, need for laparotomy

TAH (total abdominal hysterectomy): Bleeding, infection, trauma to pelvic organs including bowel, bladder, nerves, vessels, future prolapse

Vaginal hysterectomy: Bleeding, infection, pain, trauma to pelvic organs (including bowel, bladder, ureters, nerves, vessels), future prolapse, vaginal diameter changes

Version: Fetal distress resulting in need for urgent caesarean section, rupture of membranes, failure

Vesicovaginal fistulas: Bleeding, infection, trauma to pelvic organs including bowel, bladder, ureter, failure of procedure

Vulvectomy: Bleeding, infection, pain, need for lymph node dissection, wound breakdown

Appendix 3: Potential Complications Occurring during General Operative Procedures

Complications occur mainly due to:

- anaesthesia
- positioning of the patient
- the distension media
- the operative procedure
- delayed complication
- failure of the procedure (persistent symptoms).

ANAESTHETIC COMPLICATIONS: there is a risk to the patient's health in most procedures (minor or major complications). These complications are similar to those associated with most procedures undertaken under general anaesthetics.

Specific complication in hysteroscopic surgery is due to shock resulting from either perforation of the uterus, damage to major vessels or fluid overload. Consequences due to these complications are more immediately evident to the anaesthetist. Discontinuation of the procedure and return to the supine position (if not already done so) to provide immediate resuscitation will be carried out.

POSITIONING OF PATIENTS: incorrect positioning of the patient on the operative table may result in:

- nerve injury (lateral popliteal, peroneal nerve). Pressure on the peroneal nerve is the most common nerve injury especially during vaginal surgery. This is caused by pressure on the lateral side of the leg during the lithotomy position, resulting in paraesthesia and foot drop. To avoid this complication pressure should not be applied between the lithotomy poles and legs by using padding. The padded gutter is better to hold the leg.
- brachial plexus injury. This can occur from incorrect positioning of the shoulder during the Trendelenberg position. Abduction of the arm on arm board for venous access can cause compression of the nerve causing paraesthesia. (If there is a suspicion of nerve damage then an opinion from a neurologist should be sought before discharge from the hospital.)
- back injury
- damage to the soft tissue
- deep venous thrombosis (DVT)
- damage to the hip, shoulder, and knee joint.

BACK INJURIES: The anaesthetised patient is defenceless against traction injury to the lumbar spine. The legs should always be lifted simultaneously and kept together until they are at the appropriate height, when they should be abducted gently and placed in the supports. They should never be over-abducted as this can lead to damage of the sacro-iliac joints.

DAMAGE TO SOFT TISSUES: It is the responsibility of the surgeon to ensure that no part of the patient is in contact with metal parts of the table because these can act as return plates for electrical energy and burns can occur at the point of contact.

DEEP VENOUS THROMBOSIS: Deep venous thrombosis can also result from prolonged compression of the calves by the leg supports. The surgeon should ensure that the type of support is appropriate and well padded. If DVT is suspected the advice of a physician should be sought and appropriate anticoagulant therapy instituted immediately.

Appendix 4: Complications of Radiotherapy

Early complications (up to 3–6 months)
- Tiredness (may last weeks to months)
- Skin reaction (dry erythema, moist desquamation, dilated capillaries)
- Oral mucositis and oral thrush
- Nausea and vomiting (brain and abdominal irradiation)
- Diarrhoea (mainly abdominal pelvic irradiation)
- Dysphagia (thoracic irradiation)
- Cystitis, haematuria (pelvic irradiation)
- Bone marrow suppression leading to anaemia, neutropenia, thrombocytopenia, infection (both bacterial and fungal)
- Lactational impairment
- Acute radiation pneumonitis

Late reaction (more than 6 months)
- Lymphoedema
- Fat necrosis
- Soft tissue fibrosis and contracture
- CNS system (somnolence, spinal cord myelopathy,) brachial plexopathy (after breast cancer radiotherapy)
- Respiratory system (cough, dysnoea, lung fibrosis, fracture of ribs)
- Gastro-intestinal system (xerostomia, alteration in taste sensation, benign stricture of the bowel, fistula)
- Genito-urinary system (fibrosis and urethral stricture, infertility, amenorrhea, premature ovarian failure, vaginal stenosis, dyspareaunia, impotence)
- Cardiovascular system (impairment of cardiac function)
- Endocrinal system (panhypopituitarism, hypothyroidism)
- Impairment of immune system (opportunistic infection)
- Cataracts
- Secondary cancers (sarcoma, AML)

Appendix 5: Complications of Chemotherapy

As a procedure
- Extravasation (pain, thrombosis, tissue necrosis, skin ulceration, necrosis to deeper structure)
- Pneumothorax
- Mediastinal bleeding
- Infection

As a result of chemotherapeutic agent
- GI toxicity (anorexia, nausea, vomiting, dehydration, weakness, weight loss, structural damage – malabsorbtion, gastrointestinal bleeding)
- Haematological toxicity (due to suppression of major cell lines (neutropenia 4–6 hours, thrombocytopenia 5–7 days, anaemia 120 days, infection gram negative bacteria, staphylococcal and fungal)
- Oral toxicity (mucositis, thrush, xerostomia, alteration of taste sensation, pain, tooth decay)
- Dermatological toxicity (alopecia, hyperpigmentation, nail disorder, acral erythemia)
- Gonadal toxicity (gonadal failure, infertility, early menopause)
- Occular toxicity (cataract and retinitis)
- Cardio myopathy
- Hepatic toxicity (hepatitis, liver failure, veno-occlusive disease of liver)
- Renal toxicity (scarring of kidney, haematuria, cystitis, renal failure)
- Neurological toxicity (infection, leukoencephalopathy)
- Musculoskeletal toxicity (myopathy, myosistis, osteoporosis, avascular necrosis)
- Immuno-suppression
- Secondary carcinoma Hodgkin's lymphoma, non-Hodgkin's lymphoma, leukaemia

Appendix 6: Medication and Common Exposures during Pregnancy – Counselling about Risks

Medication use during pregnancy is a common concern for many patients, doctors and other healthcare providers. The effects of many medications, both prescription and over-the-counter (OTC), are difficult to quantify in some cases. In addition, as almost 50% of pregnancies are unplanned, many women take medications inadvertently before they even know they are pregnant.

Some well-known teratogens (such as thalidomide and retinoic acid) lead to clearly defined malformation syndromes.

There are a whole host of medications for which data is scarce. Consequently it is difficult to predict their impact on pregnancy.

Questions about medication use arise frequently during pregnancy, and obstetricians find themselves providing counselling about risks based on very little information in the literature. There is a great need for long-term surveillance and research on the impact of medication used during pregnancy. There are many resources currently available to assist with risk assessment and counselling.

Other Resources

The OTIS website offers fact sheets that answer frequently asked questions about common exposures (http://www.otispregnancy.org/otis-fact-sheets-s13037). Fact sheets are also available on medications (including prozac and flagyl), as well as herbal products (including echinacea and St. John's wort), vaccines, infections (including chicken pox, cytomegalovirus, toxoplasmosis), maternal medical conditions (diabetes and nausea and vomiting in pregnancy), illicit substances (cocaine), and other exposures (including caffeine, hair treatments, and shot tubs). The information sheet can be printed out on one page and is an invaluable first-line resource that can be given to patients with particular concerns.

Information is also provided regarding many common exposures and teratogenic agents e.g. thalidomide, alcohol, smoking, drugs, herbs and stress.

Genetic Counselling

Although the information provided above can help educate patients and providers, there are certain instances for which the risk assessment is particularly difficult to research or the risk of the medication or exposure is deemed to be great. In this case, genetic counselling is recommended to review the clinical situation and the exposure history and to provide detailed personalised risk assessment and counselling.

When an exposure does occur, fears can be allayed in many cases or real risks ascertained through access to appropriate information and counselling.

Drugs	Indications	Side Effects
Tamoxifen	Breast cancer (oestrogen receptor positive tumours)	Hot flushes, in pre-menstrual women: vaginal atrophy, dryness and loss of libido Long-term: endometrial hyperplasia and increased risk of carcinoma of the endometrium
Tranexamic acid (inhibits fibrinolysis)	Menorrhagia	Nausea, vomiting, diarrhoea, thromboembolic events
Danazol	Endometriosis, mammary dysplasia, gynaecomastia, menorrhagia menstrual disorders, pre-operative thinning of endometrium	Weight gain, depression, photosensitivity, nausea, menstrual disturbances, flushing, acne, hirsutism, thrombotic events
Clomiphene	Anovulatory infertility	Ovarian hyperstimulation, hot flushes, breast discomfort, abdominal distension, nausea, vomiting, depression

Drugs	Indications	Side Effects
Oestrogen	Oral contraception, treatment of menopausal symptoms, atrophic vulvovaginal conditions, atrophic endometritis, HRT	Nausea, abdominal cramps, breast enlargement, sodium and fluid retention, weight gain, headache, migraine, cholestatic jaundice, altered blood lipids, rashes, dizziness, thrombosis, hypertension
Progesterone	Oral contraception dysfunctional uterine bleeding, dysmenorrhoea, premenstrual tension, endometriosis, amenorrhoea, recurrent miscarriage, HRT	Nausea, headache, depression, hirsutism, skin reactions, weight change, increase in blood pressure
Mefenamic acid (prostaglan din synthetase inhibitor)	Dysmenorrhoea, menorrhagia	Gastro-intestinal discomfort, diarrhoea, rashes, thrombocytopenia, drowsiness
GNRH analogues (Goserelin)	Breast cancer, endometriosis, fibroids, infertility	Menopausal-like syndrome, decrease in trabecular bone density, headache, withdrawal bleeding

Table 13: Complications of common drugs used in obstetrics and gynaecology

Appendix: 7 Jehovah's Witness Blood Product and Technique Consent/Decline Checklist (©California Department of Public Health)

My signature below indicates that I request no blood derivatives other than the ones which I have designated in this consent be administered to me during this hospitalization.

My attending physician_____ has reviewed and fully explained
to me **the risks and benefits** of the following blood products and methods for alternative non-blood medical management and blood conservation available to me. My attending physician_____ has also **fully explained to me the potential risks associated by not authorizing blood and/or non blood management during this hospitalization.**

	ACCEPT	DO NOT ACCEPT
COMPONENTS OF HUMAN BLOOD		
Red Blood Cells	_____	_____
Fresh Frozen Plasma	_____	_____
Platelets	_____	_____
Cryoprecipitate	_____	_____
Albumin	_____	_____
Plasma Protein Fraction	_____	_____
INTRAVENOUS FLUIDS WHICH ARE NOT COMPONENTS OF HUMAN BLOOD		
Hetastarch	_____	_____
Balanced Salt Solutions	_____	_____
MEDICATIONS WHICH CONTAIN A FRACTION OF HUMAN BLOOD		
Rhogam	_____	_____
Erythropoetin	_____	_____
Human Immunoglobulin	_____	_____
Tisseel	_____	_____

TECHNIQUES FOR BLOOD CONSERVATION/PROCESSING

Hemodilution _____ _____
Cell Saver _____ _____

Autologous Banked Blood _____ _____
Cardiopulmonary Bypass _____ _____
Chest Drainage
Autotransfusion _____ _____
Plasmapheresis _____ _____
Hemodialysis _____ _____
Other _____ _____

PLEASE CIRCLE WHICH ONE APPLIES

I do (do not) have a durable power of attorney.
I accept (do not accept) this consent as an addendum to my durable
power of attorney.

I fully understand the options available to me and hereby release the
hospital, its personnel, the attending physician and any other person
participating in my care from any responsibility whatsoever for
unfavorable reactions or any untoward results due to my decision not
to permit the use of blood or its derivatives. The possible risks and
consequences of such refusal on my part have been fully explained
to me by my
attending physician. I fully understand such risks and consequences
may occur as a result of my decision.

DATE:_____ **TIME:**_____

SIGNATURE:_____
(patient/parent/guardian/conservator)

RELATIONSHIP:_____

WITNESS:_____